I WILL BUILD MY CHURCH

Illustrated by
Norman Guthrie Rudolph

I Will Build My Church

By Amy Morris Lillie

The Westminster Press
PHILADELPHIA

Printed in the United States of America
at The Lakeside Press
R. R. Donnelley & Sons Company, Chicago
and Crawfordsville, Indiana

CONTENTS

How the Story Began

MICHAEL came in with such a rush that the door closed behind him with a bang.

"The wind must be strong tonight," said Mother, as he poked his head into the living room.

"I guess I did slam the door," admitted Michael with a grin. "Excuse it, please. Where's Father?"

"He's working—in the dining room," said Joan, looking up from a tussle with Midge, the puppy.

"Michael," called Father, "would you like to look at these plans for the new church?"

"I want to see the plans too!" cried Joan, jumping up and running into the dining room after Michael. Midge, tucked between Joan's shoulder and cheek, licked her ear and the tip of her nose with his pink tongue.

Mother put down her sewing and followed. "The whole family may as well have a look," she said as they gathered around the table.

"It doesn't look much like a church." Joan was puzzled by the careful diagrams on Father's drawing board and the blueprints scattered over the table.

"You have to use a little imagination," said Michael loftily. "These are only plans for the builders to work by. They're not supposed to be a picture of a church."

"Wait a moment," said Father. "Let me show you. Joan, please put Midge where he can't chew on my papers."

Midge yapped sadly when Joan dropped him under the table, but he soon went to sleep with his nose on her foot.

"Now," said Father, pointing with his ruler, "this is the entrance into the vestibule which runs across the width of the church. And these are the doors leading into the center and two side aisles." As he went on to explain, even Joan began to have a picture in her mind of what the new church would look like.

"You see, Joan," Father finished, leaning back in his chair, "this is like a skeleton, which doesn't look or act like a man until it has muscles and flesh and skin on it. The builders will make my plan into a church, but the plans have to come first."

"Even when the builders have put the last stone in place and every bit of the work is done," said Mother, "it still will not be a church until something else is added."

"Do you mean people, Mother?" asked Michael. "It wouldn't be a church without people, would it?"

"That's why we are still a church," Father joined in, "even though we have had to carry on in the school building since the church burned down."

"Where was the very first church?" Joan asked.

"The first *Christian* church was just a group of people who met in an upper room of a house in Jerusalem," answered Father.

"You mean Peter and John and the rest of the disciples—after Jesus had gone away?" Michael broke in.

"Yes," said Father. "Our church is part of the one great Church of Jesus Christ which had its beginning then."

"I'd like to know how the Church began," said Joan. "Can you tell us about it, Father?"

"I'd need help for that story," Father replied. "Let's see— Mr. Wells is coming over here to look at these plans. Perhaps he can tell us a little of the Church's story."

"Oh, yes!" cried Joan, leaning over to pick up Midge, whom she had kicked off her toe in her excitement.

"Yes," echoed Michael. "Mr. Wells is a good storyteller."

All the boys and girls liked their young minister, and when he arrived, Joan and Michael could hardly wait to tell him what they had been talking about.

"Let's not be in too much of a hurry," said Mr. Wells, laughing a little at their eager questions. "The story of the Church covers nearly two thousand years. We can't tell it in a few words. How would you like a Church story hour every week or two?"

"Oh, I'd like that," Joan's eyes sparkled. "May I ask Ann?"

"And Don—and the rest of our gang?" Michael chimed in.

"Anyone—and as many as you please," said Mr. Wells.

"They can all come here," Mother suggested. "We could make it right after dinner on Friday, when there are no lessons for the next day. Would that be all right for you, Mr. Wells?"

"Next Friday evening will be just the time to begin our story," said Mr. Wells, "for Sunday will be the seventh Sunday after Easter—the day the Church remembers its birthday."

"Ann goes to St. Paul's Church," said Joan; "does that make any difference?"

"Not a bit," Mr. Wells answered.

1. The Upper Room

It was Friday evening. Joan and Ann were curled up on the couch with Midge between them, while Michael and Don had their heads together over a ship model that they had been making. Father sat in his big chair, and Mother, in her usual place beside the table, was knitting a sweater for Joan.

Mr. Wells came in with some of the other boys and girls. "This might be a group of the early followers of Jesus," he said, looking around the room. "Mothers and fathers, boys and girls, and often a neighbor or two, met together in those days just as we are doing tonight."

"If we were early Christians our house would be different," said Joan. "It would have a flat roof, and steps on the outside going up to the second floor. I saw a picture of one last Sunday."

"We'd be wearing tunics," added Michael, "and Father would probably have a beard!"

When everybody had found a seat, Mr. Wells turned toward the open window. "Let's try to imagine," he said, "that we can look through this window and watch what the followers of Jesus in Jerusalem were doing those first days after he had left them."

SPRING sunshine was hot and bright on the hills of Judea. It made the golden roof of the Temple gleam, and spilled over the city walls into valleys where the farmers were harvesting their small fields of ripe wheat. When the grain had been safely stored away,

11

they would be ready to celebrate a day of thanksgiving called the Feast of Pentecost.

Peter and John came out of the cool shade of an olive orchard and stopped for a moment to watch the busy workers in the fields. They were young men with sunburned skin and strong shoulders, showing that they too were used to working in the sun.

"We raise better wheat in Galilee," said John. "The soil of Judea is poor even in the valleys."

"There is no wheat anywhere like that which grows around Capernaum," said Peter.

"I wonder," said John, "if we shall ever go back to our homes in Galilee."

"That must be as God wills," said Peter. "The Master gave us a great work to do, John. Before he left us he said we must wait in Jerusalem until God sends us power to do it. We have seen his resurrection, and we will tell the good news in Jerusalem first, and throughout Judea and Samaria, and to the ends of the earth!" Peter's eyes were shining.

"When do you think this power will come, Peter?" John's eyes too were burning with excitement.

"God will choose his own time," said Peter more quietly. "We must be patient, John. Whenever the time comes, we will be ready. Now we must get back to the city. Our brothers will be expecting us."

In one of the white, flat-roofed houses of Jerusalem, Peter and John found a little company gathered. Their meeting place was a room on the upper

12

floor. Mary, the mother of Jesus, and Jesus' brothers
were there, and the rest of the men to whom Jesus
had given the name "apostle." Other friends and disciples from Galilee were also in the group, including
a few children.

Peter and John were greeted joyfully, and a young
boy ran to get a basin of water to wash the dust of
the hot roads from their feet.

"I can't forget," said Peter, as he loosened the
strap of his worn sandal, "how the Master bathed our
feet at the last supper we ate with him. I was so
ashamed when he knelt before me."

"We were all thinking only of how we could get ahead of the others, and have the place of highest honor," broke in John.

The children too wanted to tell about the Master who had been their friend. "He told such wonderful stories," said one. "I stood by his knee and he put his arm around me!" cried a second. "Jesus carved a boat for me," said a boy, drawing the little toy from the folds of his tunic and running his hand along the smooth wood.

"What I love to think about," said Mary Magdalene quickly, "is the first day of the week in the garden." Mary's face was shining with the memory of that early morning meeting with her risen Lord.

"Yes," said Peter with a smile. "When you came running back with your story, John and I could not wait for you to finish before we went hurrying off to the tomb. John got there first."

"But it was in the evening that we were sure Jesus lived," John interrupted. "As we sat here, not daring to speak, we suddenly heard the Master's greeting, 'Peace be with you,' and we knew he was here among us."

All grew very quiet, thinking of that wonderful moment. Then Mary, the mother of Jesus, spoke softly. "He promised to be with us always," she said, "even to the end of the world."

The long, slanting rays of the setting sun fell across the room, lighting up the earnest faces. Peter drew a

scroll of the Prophet Isaiah out of the box where it was kept with other Hebrew scriptures. Unrolling it, Peter read:

"'The Spirit of the Lord God is upon me;
Because the Lord hath anointed me
To preach good tidings unto the meek;
He hath sent me to bind up the broken-hearted,
To proclaim liberty to the captives,
And the opening of the prison to them that are
bound.'"

When Peter had finished reading, all prayed together that God would use them also "to preach good tidings" and give them courage and strength to do whatever he should ask. Then the little group of friends sat down to eat supper. Remembering the Master who had loved to sit at the table with them bound them close to each other.

As the Day of Pentecost dawned, pilgrims streamed into Jerusalem and great throngs climbed the steep, winding streets leading to the Temple. They came from many parts of the world, for the Jewish harvest festivals were great religious holidays.

The disciples and friends of Jesus had gathered in their usual meeting place. Later they too planned to go to the Temple. They were no longer afraid of arrest, and they wanted to take their part in this ceremony which was dear to all Jewish people.

Suddenly, in the room where they were sitting, something happened. It seemed to them that the sound of a great wind filled the place, and that a strange new fire was kindled in their hearts and minds. A feeling of great power and joy flooded over them as they knew God's Spirit was among them. They cried out in thankfulness and praise.

The sound of their voices attracted the curiosity of the crowd outside. People came running to see what had happened. When Peter saw them pressing into the courtyard, he said to the other apostles: "Come, let us speak to these people. They have come from many parts of the world and will carry the good news of Jesus back to their homes. Let us tell them of the risen Christ!"

As he faced the crowd, Peter's heart thrilled with joy, for he knew that his work for Christ had begun. His voice rang out clearly and everyone stopped to listen.

"The wonderful works which were done by Jesus of Nazareth are known to many of you," Peter said. "Some of you were here at the Feast of the Passover when he was crucified. This Jesus, who was put to death by his enemies, did not stay in the tomb. God raised him from the dead and has given him a place of honor and power in his Kingdom. Of this we are all witnesses."

Some of the people whispered together and looked as though they could not believe what Peter was saying. But Peter's next words were even more startling: "And now God has sent his Holy Spirit, that we, who are disciples of Jesus Christ, may tell of him everywhere. Let all know that God has made him both Lord and Christ, this Jesus whom you crucified!"

No wonder their faces grew pale. What a terrible thing if this were true—that the Galilean, whom they had seen die the death of a criminal, was really the Saviour of whom the prophets had spoken! They cried out anxiously to Peter and the other apostles, "Brothers, what are we to do?"

"Come and be followers of Jesus Christ with us," urged Peter. "Believe what I have told you and give up your evil ways. God will forgive you if you ask him, and you too shall receive the Holy Spirit. The promise of the Spirit is not for us alone; it is for all who accept the good news of Jesus Christ and follow in his way."

The people flocked around the apostles, begging to

hear more of this Gospel, and to be counted among those who believed. Before the day was over, three thousand men and women had been added to the company of the disciples.

After Pentecost the apostles began to preach and teach without fear throughout Jerusalem. They went every day to the Temple and spoke to those who gathered in the Temple Courts. Jesus himself had taught there many times, and the apostles must have felt very sure that his Spirit was speaking through them as they preached his good news in the great colonnades of Solomon's Porch.

There were more believers every day. People called them the Nazareans because they told of Jesus, who had been known as the Nazarene. "Look," someone on the street would say to his companion, "there are some of the Nazareans. You can tell them by their joyful faces. Let's listen to what they are saying." And as they listened many were led to believe.

One day as Peter and John went into the Temple to pray, a crippled man was carried to his usual place beside the great doorway. As Peter and John drew near he begged them to give him money.

"I have no silver and gold," said Peter, "but I give you what I have; in the name of Jesus Christ of Nazareth, walk!"

As Peter took the man's hand and raised him to his feet, strength seemed to flow into his body. He jumped about in his joy, and then followed Peter and John into the Temple to praise and thank God.

News of this came to Caiaphas, the high priest.
Caiaphas remembered Jesus of Nazareth, whom he
had sent to his death. "How does it happen," he
asked, "that there are more and more followers of
the Nazarene when their leader has been crucified?"
He called the Temple guard. "Bring me these men
who have healed the cripple that I may question
them," he said. So Peter and John were arrested and
brought before Caiaphas and the rulers of the Temple.

"In whose name are you preaching and healing the
sick?" Caiaphas asked them.

Peter answered proudly: "In the name of Jesus of
Nazareth, whom you crucified, whom God raised from
the dead."

Caiaphas didn't know what to do with these men who spoke so boldly. "Beat them and let them go," he said at last, "but they must not speak again in the name of Jesus." But, in spite of the danger, Peter and John kept right on with their work.

At the close of day, when the great doors of the Temple had swung shut, the apostles walked back through the darkening streets to the upper room. Here the lamps had been lighted, and their families and friends were waiting for the evening hour of teaching and prayer. This was followed by a meal of bread and wine. When the loaf of bread was broken and passed among them, and the cup of wine was taken, all felt very close to the beloved Master who had eaten his last supper with his friends.

There were now too many believers for all to gather in the upper room, so smaller groups met in their homes. Everyone shared his money and other belongings with the rest of the brothers, as whatever happened to one was important to all. The apostles had charge of the common fund and gave to each person enough for his needs. Sometimes there were extra expenses to be met. One of the brothers had been robbed on the road to Jericho. Another had a sick child who needed special food and clothing.

One evening a number of people came to the upper room to see the apostles. "We are not being treated fairly," they complained. "You give a larger share of food and money to some than you do to us."

"We have tried to be fair," said Peter, "but if you are not satisfied, I think it would be better to choose other men who will plan for the good of all our people. Then we who are apostles can give our whole time to preaching and teaching the word of God."

This idea seemed to please everybody. Seven men were chosen and the apostles prayed for them and blessed them in their new work. One of the seven was a young man named Stephen.

Stephen's heart was on fire to tell the story of Jesus Christ. He believed it meant the beginning of a new way of life for all men everywhere. Besides helping to care for the needs of the people, Stephen gave much of his time to preaching.

"God cares more about what is in your minds and hearts," Stephen told his listeners, "than he does about the religious laws you obey so carefully. What you do may be right according to the Law, but your hearts are filled with greed and unkindness."

A day came when Stephen, like Peter and John, stood before the high priest and rulers of the Temple. Stephen did not answer the charges made against him, for he knew they were only an excuse to have him punished. He spoke plainly to those who accused him. "Your fathers have broken the law of God over and over again all through their history," he said. "But you have broken that law most of all by putting God's Son to death."

This made his accusers so angry that they dragged

Stephen outside the city gate and stoned him to death. As he was dying, Stephen, like Jesus, prayed for his murderers: "Lord, do not hold this sin against them."

Watching this cruel scene was a young Jew whose Roman name was Paul. He came from Tarsus, a city of Asia Minor. His father was a Roman citizen, but Paul had been trained to know and to keep strictly the Law of Moses. He too was sure that Stephen was an enemy of all he believed to be true and sacred. As Paul watched Stephen die, he was coldly making plans to imprison or destroy all of these Nazareans who threatened the religion handed down from Moses and the Prophets.

Paul soon began a violent attack upon the church, and men, women, and children fled from Jerusalem into all parts of Palestine and even beyond. But, like sparks from a great explosion which fly in every direction and set new fires, the scattering of the Nazareans carried the Gospel to many distant cities. Wherever believers found a place of safety, they began to tell all they had seen and learned of the Gospel of Jesus Christ.

Joan drew a long breath. "I feel sorry about Stephen," she said soberly. "How could people be so cruel?"

"They were very angry," said Mr. Wells, "and angry people often do things they are ashamed of later. Then, too, these people were sure that what Stephen taught was wrong."

"Do you know what I think?" said Don. "I think Paul must have been the very sorriest of all when he found out that everything Stephen had said was true."

"Paul changed his mind about many things," said Mr. Wells, "but that's a story for another time."

Joan drew a big breath. "The story's going on and on—"

"Why, it's just begun!" said Michael.

2. Good News to the Gentiles

"How would you like to go traveling tonight?" asked Mr. Wells.

"Yes!" shouted all the children in chorus.

"All right," said Mr. Wells, "but don't start to pack, because we're not taking any baggage. We won't travel by train or airplane. We'll ride a horse or a donkey, and sometimes we'll just walk. It may take us a week to go as far as a hundred and fifty miles."

"A week!" exclaimed Michael. "Why a plane could do that in less than an hour!"

"There are no planes," said Mr. Wells. "The only way we can travel is over the roads built by Roman slaves, for we're going on a journey with Paul."

Again and again Paul had broken into the homes of the followers of Jesus in Jerusalem, forcing them to flee for their lives or be dragged off to prison. But lately he had been hearing that the faith preached by these Nazareans was growing in many other cities. "This must not be allowed to go on," said Paul. "I will start at Damascus. If I can destroy the new belief there, it will be easy to stamp it out in other places."

So Paul went to the high priest. "Give me a letter to the rulers in Damascus," he said, "and I will arrest any Nazareans I find there and bring them back to Jerusalem." Caiaphas was only too glad to write these letters, and Paul had them in the folds of his cloak as he led a small band of horsemen through one of the city gates and rode swiftly away to the north.

Riding along the curving shores of the Sea of Galilee, Paul's eyes followed the sails of fishing boats skimming over the blue water. "Why don't these followers of the Nazarene go back to their fishing?" he asked himself. "It is strange how this company of believers is becoming so strong!"

Then Paul thought of Stephen's death. To whom was he speaking when he said, "Lord, do not hold this sin against them"? Sin! Paul's face flushed with anger. Stephen, himself, was a sinner when he dared to speak against the Law and the Temple!

Crossing the Jordan River, Paul and his companions climbed to the highlands where the road unrolled before them like a ribbon. At last they came in sight of the city. The noonday sun was high in the heavens and Damascus looked like a beautiful garden in the distance. The journey was almost over. "Before nightfall," Paul said to his men, "we shall reach the city and hunt out these followers of the Nazarene."

Suddenly a strange thing happened. There came such a blaze of light that Paul fell to the ground blinded. Then he heard a voice saying, "Paul, Paul, why do you persecute me?" At once Paul cried out, "Who are you, Lord?" The answer came, "I am Jesus, whom you are persecuting."

"What shall I do, Lord?" asked Paul, trembling.

"Rise and enter the city, and you will be told what you are to do," was the answer.

Paul did not ride proudly into Damascus and present his letters from Caiaphas to the Jewish leaders. Instead, his companions led him, helpless as a small child, to the home of a friend. There he sat for three days without sight and without eating or drinking. Paul was sure now that everything the disciples of the Nazarene preached was true. He could understand the light he had seen on Stephen's face, and the courage of those who had been killed or imprisoned for their belief. Jesus was alive!

One day as he sat thinking of all that had happened to him, Paul felt two hands placed upon his head. Then a quiet voice said: "Brother Paul, the Lord Jesus has sent me to you. Receive your sight, and be filled with the Holy Spirit." Paul's eyes were opened. He looked up into the kind face of Ananias, a man of Damascus. "Jesus has chosen you," continued this disciple, "to be a witness for him to all people, to the Gentiles as well as the Jews."

Paul was now eager to join the people he had so bitterly persecuted. *How can I do this?* he wondered. *Who will believe me if I try to work with the very people I came to destroy?*

At first he found that very few *did* believe him. The disciples in Damascus could not understand this change in Paul and they did not trust him. Neither did those who had expected Paul to help them to crush out this new belief. They were very bitter about the way Paul was acting. "The man is a traitor," they said. "Let us find a way to get rid of him." So they plotted to kill Paul.

Guards were placed at the gates of the city to keep Paul from escaping, but his friends thought of a plan to save him. One night they lowered him down over the city wall in a basket made of rope, and he escaped in the darkness. *How different this is from the journey I had planned!* thought Paul, as he trudged along the lonely road.

When he went to Jerusalem, it was the same story. Even Peter and the other apostles found it hard to believe that Paul was really a disciple of Jesus Christ. Barnabas helped him to win their friendship, but Paul did not stay long in Jerusalem. His old friends now hated him for having become a follower of Jesus. They too wanted to kill him.

Paul felt so sure that Jesus had work for him to do in the world outside Palestine that he decided to go back to the country where he had been born. So he slipped quietly out of Jerusalem and went to a port on the shore of the Great Sea, where he took a ship and sailed north for the city of Tarsus.

Tarsus was one of the great cities of the Roman Empire. Rome ruled most of the known world, and her cities offered their blue, sunlit harbors to ships carrying traders and travelers to all parts of the world. Most of the people living in these cities were Gentiles, a name given by the Jews to people who were not Jews. For a number of years Paul carried the message of Jesus to people in the neighborhood of Tarsus, preaching to both Jews and Gentiles.

To the east of Tarsus, near the shore of the Great Sea, was another city, Antioch. Many of the believers from Jerusalem had taken refuge in Antioch after the death of Stephen. The people of Antioch saw with surprise that Gentiles and Jews were worshiping together and telling of One whom they called Christ. "They are Christians," people would say to one another as they passed them on the street.

Travelers to Jerusalem were telling of the way the Christian Church at Antioch had grown. "But the Gentile Christians do not always want to observe the customs of the Jews," they would say. This troubled the apostles. They realized that Gentile Christians might not think that keeping the Law was important. "It would be too bad," James told Peter, "if the believers at Antioch should be divided by these arguments. The Gospel of Jesus is meant to bind people together, not to separate them."

One day Peter came striding into Antioch and was welcomed with joy by Barnabas and Paul, who were teaching there. Peter had been shown in a dream that every nation and all people are dear to God. So, when he came to Antioch, he sat at the table where Gentiles and Jews ate their evening meal together.

But there were men from Jerusalem who believed that Jesus had come to save only the Jews and who made Peter feel that he must give up the friendly custom of eating with the Gentiles. They would not listen when Paul tried to tell them that many Gen-

tiles were already following the way of Christ. "No!"
they cried. "We do not want these foreign people in
the Church. They must obey the Law of Moses before we can accept them as Christians." Later the
leaders of the Church in Jerusalem decided that
Peter and the other apostles should continue to work
among the Jews, while Paul and his helpers would
be free to preach to the Gentiles.

About this time Paul started on the journeys that
would take him to most of the big cities of the Roman
world bordering on the Great Sea. Along highways,
over mountains, or by ship from one port to another,
he traveled. He was carrying richer treasure than
were the plodding camel caravans that passed him,
and it was to be given freely to all men. The Gospel
of Jesus Christ was the treasure he had for the
world, and it was all he cared about.

One day Paul and his friend Silas crossed the snow-
covered mountains and followed the Roman road to

Lystra. As they drew near the city gate, Paul and Silas could see the Temple of Zeus, the greatest of the Roman gods. Paul told Silas the story of his first visit. "We had healed a cripple," he said, "and the temple priests were sure that we were gods."

"Wasn't it here too that you were stoned?" asked Silas.

"Yes," answered Paul, who remembered only too well how the heavy rocks felt as they beat him to the ground. "Some of our own Jewish people stirred up a mob against us. They left me for dead outside the city gate." Paul's face was sad as he added, "I thought of the day Stephen was stoned."

A young man ran to meet Paul and Silas as they entered the city. This was Timothy, whom Paul loved as his own son. Timothy's family had become Christians during Paul's former visit to Lystra.

"I must carry the Gospel to the great cities of the west," said Paul to Timothy and his family later. "I would like Timothy to go with me."

Timothy's eyes were shining as he looked at his mother and father. "We are very proud that our son can be of help to you, Paul," answered Timothy's parents. "We put him in your care."

A few days later Paul, Silas, and Timothy started out. They traveled westward, preaching and teaching as they went, until they came to the shore beyond which lay Greece and Rome. There Paul had a dream, which he felt was a message from God, telling him to cross over into the cities of Greece. Soon many of these cities—Philippi, Athens, Corinth—heard the voices of Paul and his friends. They met people wherever they could—by the riverside, in the house of a friend, in a school or synagogue.

Paul was often hungry and cold, he was beaten and put in prison again and again, but he never thought of giving up his work. Through it all Timothy was his loyal friend and faithful messenger. "Timothy, my true child in the faith," Paul called him.

In all his travels Paul and his companions never forgot the Church at Jerusalem. Whenever there was hunger or need, the churches in the north shared with their brothers in Jerusalem. These gifts were a bond among them all, whether or not they thought alike about their laws and customs. It was to take such gifts that Paul went back to Jerusalem for the last time.

The apostles welcomed Paul and praised him for his work among the Gentiles, as well as for the gifts he brought. But there were still people who wanted to make trouble for him, and Paul was arrested. After many months in prison he claimed the right of a Roman citizen to a trial under Caesar, the emperor. So Paul finally arrived in Rome a prisoner. He made the long journey by boat, sailing for many weeks on the Great Sea. The voyage nearly ended in shipwreck, but one spring day Paul and his faithful friends sailed into a beautiful Italian bay. Some days later they entered the great city.

"What happened when Paul was shipwrecked?" asked Don.

"It's an exciting story," said Mr. Wells. "Luke, who was with Paul on the voyage, tells it better than I can. Suppose you look for it in the twenty-seventh and twenty-eighth chapters of the book of The Acts of the Apostles. The important thing is that Paul was saved. The Christians in Rome were to need his courage and faith in the hard days which were ahead."

3. The Church Is Tested

"If this nice weather keeps up," said Father, "the foundations of the church will be ready in no time."

"Isn't there a hymn about the Church's foundation?" asked Joan.

"Yes," said Mr. Wells. "The hymn says that the Church's one Foundation is Jesus Christ her Lord. Paul said the same thing in one of his letters."

"We read about Paul's shipwreck," said Michael. "Mother, Father, and all of us. Paul was brave, and he told the rest what to do. He saved their lives."

"Yes, he did," said Mr. Wells. "But now let's see what happened after Paul got to Rome."

THE Tiber River, swollen by spring rains in the mountains, swirled between hills and under bridges as it flowed through the city. From one of the bridges Paul looked down on boats and barges bringing cargoes from Ostia, the seaport for Rome. The shoulders of the boatmen were bent as they strained at their oars in the swift current. They were bringing grain from Egypt, wine and olive oil from Greece and Spain, spices from the East, and many other good things.

Paul turned to look up at the hills on which the city was built. On one he could see the emperor's palace; on another the white-columned Temple of Jupiter gleamed against the sky. He had seen the young emperor, Nero, riding in a triumphal procession up the winding road to the Temple. Nero was worshiped as a god by the Roman people. *How long will it be, he wondered, before Nero gives me my freedom?*

As Paul walked on through the streets of Rome, the rattle of the chain on his wrist and the clanking sword of the Roman soldier at his side reminded him always that he was a prisoner. But he held his head high. *I am a prisoner*, he thought, *because I preach the Gospel of Christ. I am not ashamed of these chains, nor am I afraid of what men can do to me.*

Paul did not let being a prisoner interfere with his work. The Roman officers allowed him to live in his own rented house under guard. There he preached the message of Jesus with fire and zeal. To his house came the poor and oppressed who longed for new hope. People of wealth and importance, who were not satisfied with the worship of Roman gods, also came to listen to him. Some came even from the emperor's household.

Other old friends joined Paul in Rome. One day his heart was gladdened by the arrival of his young friend, Timothy, and John Mark, one of Paul's first helpers. They brought news from the other churches. Paul had not forgotten the Christians in the churches he had started. He sent them encouragement and advice by messengers or in letters. He could not write easily because of the chain on his wrist. So Timothy wrote most of his letters for him. Sometimes he had to reprove his friends for falling into ways that were not true to the Gospel of Christ. In other letters he praised them for their good works. But Paul wrote always with a loving heart and a spirit of helpfulness.

Far away in Philippi, where Paul had started a church ten years before, his friends were thinking of him. They knew he was a prisoner in Rome and were afraid he might not have all he needed for his health and comfort. They decided they would like to send gifts to him. Although Paul was used to earning enough money to take care of himself, this kind thought of his friends at Philippi touched his heart. He asked for Timothy's help once more and wrote a beautiful letter to them.

This was one of the last letters written by Paul. In just a short time he was to give his life for the Gospel of Jesus Christ. It was a loving letter. "I thank my God when I remember you," he wrote. "I hold you all in my heart as partners with me."

Timothy's reed pen scratched along as Paul walked back and forth, telling his friends of his hopes and prayers for them and urging them to "stand firm in the Lord." No wonder Paul's friends kept his letters and read them over and over again when they needed to be brave and strong!

"He must have written a great many letters," said Joan, thinking how hard it was for her to write just one!

"Paul's letters make up a large part of the New Testament," answered Mr. Wells.

The Christians were now increasing so rapidly that they could not go unnoticed, even in Rome, where there were many kinds of worship. There were things about them that people could not understand.

At first the Romans thought the Christians had the same religion as the Jews. Paul was a Jew, and Jesus, whose Gospel he preached, had been a Jew. Rome was used to the Jews. There were synagogues where Jews worshiped their one God, and they were the only people in the Roman Empire who were not compelled to burn incense to the emperor. But the Christians soon showed that they were different. There were more Gentiles than Jews among them. Not only did they refuse to worship the emperor, but they would not follow other Roman customs. "We must look into this," said the Romans. So Christians were spied upon, and many foolish and untrue stories about them were passed around from one person to another.

"They have secret meetings when they eat together," whispered one. "I have heard that they eat human flesh. These people must be cannibals!" In some way the words said by Jesus at his last supper with the disciples had come to the ears of these men. Jesus had said: "This bread is my body. This wine is my blood." So the Romans thought that real flesh and blood were being eaten.

There were other ways in which Christians were different. They did not send their children to school, because the lessons were about gods in whom they did not believe. Then, too, they did not enjoy the things that gave pleasure to the Romans. Christians did not like to watch slaves and prisoners of war fight with wild beasts in the arena. They believed in treating their slaves kindly. Greek and Roman plays also seemed cruel and wicked, so Christians would not go to the theater, which was one of Rome's chief amusements. Altogether, the Romans thought the Christians were a very strange company. The worst of it was that they were drawing Greeks and Romans away from the temples of pagan gods.

"The gods will be angry and punish us if we let these people live!" cried the Romans, and they began to blame everything unpleasant that happened on the Christians. To be a Christian meant being under suspicion.

A fire broke out in Rome. It burned for a week and almost destroyed the whole city. Nero said the Christians started the fire. Many of them were nailed to crosses and burned. Up on the hill, in the garden of his palace, Nero watched these human torches light up the night sky.

This was the beginning of a very terrible persecution of the Christians in Rome. It is not certain just when Paul died, but we do know that when the day came, he went without fear to give his life for Jesus

Christ. "I have fought the good fight, I have finished the race, I have kept the faith," Paul wrote to Timothy before he died.

For a long time things looked very dark for the Church. Men, women, and children were forced to hide, and no home in the city was safe. The Christians took refuge in underground caves and tunnels on the outskirts of Rome.

In times of persecution Christians went creeping along these narrow, winding passages, some as deep as seventy feet below the surface, to their secret places for worship. The pale light of a lamp flickered over their tired faces as the leader read from the Scriptures and prayed that God would help them to stand fast in these dreadful tests of their faith. As they broke bread and drank the cup of wine together, comfort and strength came to them. On the walls of these caves the Christians painted pictures that stood for their beliefs. Many of these pictures became symbols that are in our Church today.

"What kind of pictures?" asked Joan.

"I think someone must have painted a shepherd with a lamb in his arms," answered Mr. Wells. "It would have helped in those days of suffering to remember Jesus as the Good Shepherd who would always take care of his sheep."

"We have a window in our church that has a picture of the Good Shepherd," said Ann.

For more than two hundred years the Roman Empire tried to destroy the Christians. Six years after the burning of Rome, Jerusalem was taken and the Temple was in ruins. The Jewish Christians were scattered all over the known world.

In the cities where Paul and his friends began their work new leaders were carrying on. With an unfriendly government looking for any excuse to punish Christians, it took strong leaders to keep the Church together. Christians turned to their leaders for advice and help. There were teachers who were called bishops or elders, and deacons who took care of the needs of the people for food, clothing, and shelter. Later the bishops had charge of many small churches, with elders to help them. As the years passed, some bishops, such as those at Rome in the West and Alexandria in the East, came to be considered more important than others.

Many of the Early Church leaders were men of great courage. At Antioch there was a bishop named Ignatius. Like Paul, Ignatius was a great letter writer and wrote many letters to the churches. He too was kind and patient and earnest in his work for Christ. But at last Ignatius was taken to Rome where he was thrown to the wild beasts in the arena.

Ignatius had a very dear friend, Polycarp, who was also a bishop. Polycarp was an old man when he was burned at the stake in Smyrna. "Say that Caesar is Lord, and save your life," the soldiers told Polycarp.

But Polycarp would not deny the Christ whom he had served so long and faithfully.

A scholar named Justin went to Rome where he wrote an appeal to the emperor to treat Christians with justice. Justin explained much that was not understood about the Christians, and he showed how untrue were the stories told about them. He said: "The Christians are not against the government. They respect the law like anyone else. They pray for the emperor, even though they will not worship him. The religion of Jesus Christ makes people citizens of the Kingdom of God, where God alone is the ruler. They cannot worship any other gods."

Justin's writings did not do much to change the emperor, but the Christians themselves read what he had written and were ready to die for their faith. Justin, like Ignatius and Polycarp, was put to death.

Sometimes the Church was allowed to grow in peace. Roman emperors were too much interested in their own affairs and pleasures to think about religion unless something happened that seemed dangerous to their rule. There were large groups of Christians in southern Gaul, Spain, North Africa and Egypt.

So many people wanted to give up pagan religions and become Christians that it was necessary for the Church to be sure they really were in earnest. Each one had to be taught carefully what this step meant. First of all he had to say what he believed. The Latin word for "I believe" is *credo*, so this statement of belief was called a creed. The creed was put in simple words, something like these:

I believe in God the Father, Maker of heaven
    and earth.
And in Jesus Christ, His only Son, who was
    crucified and rose again.
I believe in the Holy Spirit;
    the holy catholic Church; the forgiveness of sins;
    and life everlasting.

After saying what he believed, a new member was expected to confess his sins and repent of them. Each new believer was baptized by the bishop or minister as a sign that his sins had been washed away.

Baptism was more than a sign of cleansing from sin and of God's forgiveness. It was also a sacrament.

47

The word sacrament means a vow or pledge. In baptism the Christian promised to serve God and follow the way of the Lord Jesus Christ.

Another sacrament was the Lord's Supper. In the early days of the Church the Lord's Supper had been a separate meal. Now it was celebrated at every worship service. Services began with Scripture reading, which was followed by a sermon. Then the congregation joined in prayers and singing. At the end all shared in the sacred bread and wine of the Lord's Supper, served to them by their leader. Then an offering was taken for those who were in need.

Church services were no longer held on the Jewish Sabbath. They had been changed to the first day of the week, which Christians called the Lord's Day. This was because Jesus had risen on the first day of the week after his crucifixion.

Many years had passed without any terrible persecution, but suddenly the time of peace ended. Decius was emperor, and Rome was about to celebrate a birthday—the city was a thousand years old. But things had not been going very well in the Empire. Hordes of barbarians were pushing their way down from the north, and the Roman legions were fighting to force them back. Decius was sure that Rome was having this trouble because the old gods of the Empire had been neglected and were angry. People everywhere, he said, must at once offer sacrifices and pray to the gods to give Rome once again the power to win in all battles, and to conquer the enemy.

"The Christians are more to blame than anyone else!" cried Decius. "They will not fight for Rome or worship the emperor. We will force them to sacrifice like the rest or they will be imprisoned and tortured."

Then began the worst persecution the Christians had endured. Many died for their faith. Some gave way under torture, and either offered sacrifices to pagan gods or paid the priests to say they had done so. When the worst was over, those who had failed wanted to come back into the Church. There was a great outcry over this. The bishop of Rome finally ruled that they could be received again after they had repented by prayer and fasting.

Later the Church was to suffer a last great trial. Then an emperor of Rome became a Christian himself and put an end to such cruelty. All through these years the Church was being tested, and in the end it proved itself able to resist and grow because its strength was the love of Jesus Christ. "Love bears all things, endures all things," Paul had written. "Love never fails."

"I wonder if we could stand tests like that today," said Mother.

"I wouldn't like it," Michael admitted thoughtfully.

"People are giving their lives to carry on the work of Christ's Church in many parts of the world today," said Mr. Wells. "We shall talk about some of them later on."

4. The Roman World Turns to the Cross

"Well," said Father, "our church is really started. We have a cornerstone."

"I never saw a cornerstone laid before," said Joan.

"I guess almost everyone in town was there," Michael spoke with pride in his voice.

"It's just as though this was the first church ever to be built," Mother agreed.

"How long was it before the Christians started to build churches?" asked Michael.

"It was nearly three hundred years before many were built," answered Mr. Wells. "It was safer for the Christians to meet quietly in their homes than in public places. But at last the emperor of Rome gave them freedom to worship wherever they pleased. The first churches were built over the homes where Christians had worshiped, or sometimes over the tombs of their martyrs. There are still old churches in Rome with the remains of a Roman house beneath them. Suppose we leave the city of Rome for a little while and see what had been happening in another big city, far to the east."

BACK and forth, from east to west and west to east, ships sailed the Great Sea. In the harbors of the large cities Roman galleys lay at anchor beside strange-looking craft from Far Eastern waters. On the docks sailors unloaded cargoes of tin from British mines side by side with silk from China and cotton goods from India. Of all the Mediterranean ports, none was busier than Alexandria. Only Rome was larger and more important. Sailors watched eagerly for the shining beacon of Alexandria's lighthouse to guide them safely into the harbor. It rose nearly four hundred feet above the island of Pharos at the entrance to the harbor, and it was the greatest lighthouse in the world.

Alexandria was a city with marble buildings set in beautiful parks and gardens. It was well known for its men of science and learning. Three hundred years before the birth of Jesus, its scholars had discovered the secrets of the stars, had measured the size of the earth, and made maps of the world of their day. The museum and university of Alexandria were famous, and the library was the largest in the Roman Empire.

Many Jews from Palestine had settled in Alexandria, and they had brought with them their sacred books, so the Hebrew Scriptures were well known. Here the Old Testament had been translated into Greek, and here, in the early days of Christianity, messengers had brought the good news of Jesus.

In a city of so much learning it was natural that there should be schools to teach different kinds of religions. Young Christians were confused by having so many kinds of teaching all around them, so a

Christian school was formed. A pupil in this school, whose name was Origen, became its head when he was only eighteen. It happened because a persecution had killed many Christian leaders or driven them out of the city.

When the persecution came to an end, Origen gathered together what was left of the school and carried on the Christian teaching. He was a hard worker and never stopped to think about his own needs. He earned his living by copying manuscripts, but he didn't have much use for money for he went barefoot, ate very little, and slept on the ground. He spent most of every day studying the Bible, and he came to know it better than any other scholar of the Early Church.

For Christians the Old Testament was no longer the whole Bible. Other books had been written. Some of these the Church leaders had long accepted as a true record of what the disciples remembered and believed about Jesus. But there were other books they could not accept. It was many years before the complete list of books, known as the New Testament, was agreed upon. Origen's studies helped the Church to decide which books rightly belonged in this list, which was called the canon of the New Testament. Because he was not afraid to say what he believed to be true, Origen, like other Church leaders, suffered great cruelty and persecution.

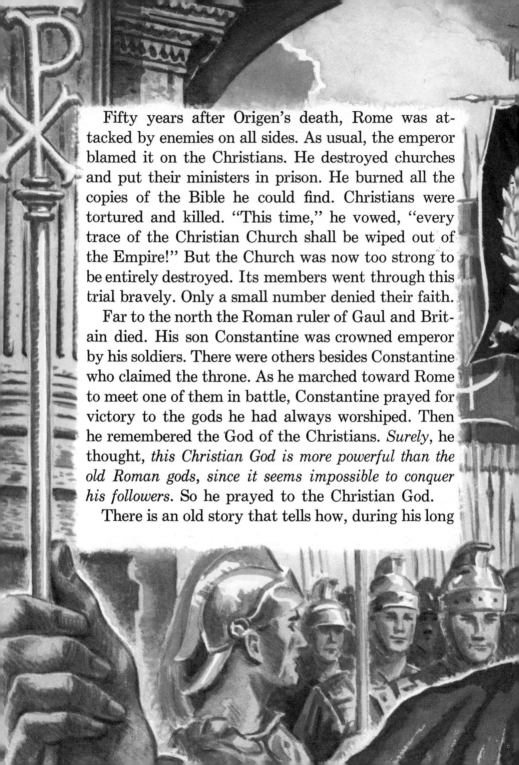

Fifty years after Origen's death, Rome was attacked by enemies on all sides. As usual, the emperor blamed it on the Christians. He destroyed churches and put their ministers in prison. He burned all the copies of the Bible he could find. Christians were tortured and killed. "This time," he vowed, "every trace of the Christian Church shall be wiped out of the Empire!" But the Church was now too strong to be entirely destroyed. Its members went through this trial bravely. Only a small number denied their faith.

Far to the north the Roman ruler of Gaul and Britain died. His son Constantine was crowned emperor by his soldiers. There were others besides Constantine who claimed the throne. As he marched toward Rome to meet one of them in battle, Constantine prayed for victory to the gods he had always worshiped. Then he remembered the God of the Christians. *Surely*, he thought, *this Christian God is more powerful than the old Roman gods, since it seems impossible to conquer his followers*. So he prayed to the Christian God.

There is an old story that tells how, during his long

march, Constantine saw a cross of light above the setting sun. On it were the words, "By this sign shall ye conquer." Whether this story is true or not, we know that Constantine took these words as his motto and put the Christian symbol on the banners carried by his armies. He won a victory over his enemy in a battle by the Tiber River, outside Rome. Later the other men who claimed the throne were conquered and Constantine became emperor.

Now the Christians had a friend in the emperor instead of an enemy. Constantine put an end to all persecution. It had always been hard and dangerous to be a Christian, but now the emperor was making it easy. New members flocked to this popular faith. Sunday was made a legal holiday. Churches that had been destroyed were rebuilt. Bishops and other Christian leaders were shown respect and could travel like officers of state because of the emperor's favor.

But the new members of the Church gave very little thought to what it meant to be a Christian. They did not have to prove themselves worthy as had the earlier Christians. The long period of learning the truths of the faith was not asked of them. Nor did they have to face persecution and danger for what they believed. Many became Christians just to please the emperor.

Constantine had hoped that the Christian religion would hold the people of his empire together. But

the new freedom did not seem to lead to a peaceful, friendly spirit among the Christians. Instead, there was bitterness and disagreement within the Church.

The bitterest arguments were about whether God and Christ and the Holy Spirit were one person or three. Church leaders were asking: "What shall we teach concerning these questions? The Church is sending missionaries to the barbarians. If they all teach different beliefs, what will the barbarians think?"

Constantine did not understand very clearly what the arguments were about, and he became very tired of it all. "This quarrel must stop," he said, "or there will no longer be one Church but two." He decided to call the bishops and other Church leaders together to settle such questions.

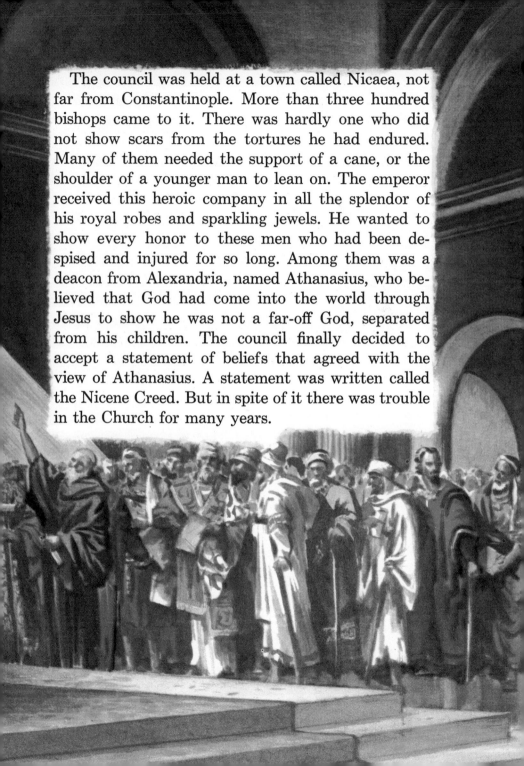

The council was held at a town called Nicaea, not far from Constantinople. More than three hundred bishops came to it. There was hardly one who did not show scars from the tortures he had endured. Many of them needed the support of a cane, or the shoulder of a younger man to lean on. The emperor received this heroic company in all the splendor of his royal robes and sparkling jewels. He wanted to show every honor to these men who had been despised and injured for so long. Among them was a deacon from Alexandria, named Athanasius, who believed that God had come into the world through Jesus to show he was not a far-off God, separated from his children. The council finally decided to accept a statement of beliefs that agreed with the view of Athanasius. A statement was written called the Nicene Creed. But in spite of it there was trouble in the Church for many years.

Constantine helped the Church in many ways, but at the same time he took away the very thing that had made it strong—the struggle against persecution. Like an athlete whose muscles grow soft when he does not use them, the Church began to lose some of its firm faith. The Roman emperors had a great deal to say in the councils of the Church, and too often the Church was a tool that the emperor used to get what he wanted.

Many Christians felt all this was wrong. But instead of trying to change it, they tried to separate themselves from it. They fled from the cities and lived a life of hardship and prayer in desert places. These men were called hermits or monks. Some of the great men of the Christian Church were monks.

"Did it make them better Christians to live by themselves?" asked Ann.

"No," Mr. Wells answered, "but it showed they were willing to give up everything for their faith. They found out that it was more Christian to help people than to run away from them. Many came back to try to make the world better."

5. The Empire Crumbles but the Church Lives On

Joan ran down to the gate to meet Ann. Midge followed on wobbly legs, his long ears flapping. "Come out in the garden," said Joan. "We're having our story out there tonight."

Don came running over from his house next door and raced across the lawn to join the rest of the boys and girls.

"We want to know more about the men who went to live in the desert," Joan said to Mr. Wells, when she had breath enough.

"All right," said Mr. Wells. "Let's see how it all started."

LONG before Constantine became a Christian emperor, a young man named Anthony in far-off Egypt was thinking about a story he had heard. The story was about a rich young ruler who was not satisfied with the way he was living. While he kept all the commandments of the Jewish Law, he felt that this was not enough. "Good Teacher, what must I do?" the young ruler asked Jesus. "Go," said Jesus, "sell all you have and give the money to the poor. Then come and follow me."

Anthony repeated these words of Jesus aloud, and his heart began to beat hard. "That is what I must do," he said, "give up everything and just follow Jesus. The rich man in the story wouldn't give up his possessions, but I will." So Anthony sold all his belongings, and after a time he left home and went out into the desert to live the life of a hermit.

Others followed Anthony's example. Soon travelers, crossing the desert by camel caravan, would see these men living alone in caves. They wore only a rough garment and ate just enough food to keep them alive. They thought that by hardship, fasting, and prayer they could escape the evils of the world.

A hermit named Pachomius decided that this was not a good kind of life. Jesus had spent his earthly life helping other people, while being a hermit meant thinking only of one's self. So Pachomius started something different. Instead of a solitary life in the desert, he and his followers lived together. They wore the same kind of clothing, and had regular hours for worship and work. They were always ready to go to the aid of travelers or to give refuge to any who were in need.

Later these men came to be called monks, and the places in which they lived, monasteries. The monks went out into the world to help the poor and sick, and to carry the good news of Christ as the early Christians had done.

In Palestine there was one monastery that stood among the hills near the little white-walled town of Bethlehem, where Jesus was born. The head of the monastery was Jerome, one of the great men of the Christian Church. Years before, he had gone from

Antioch to preach and teach in Rome. Jerome believed that people who wanted to live Christlike lives should not marry. People who wanted to marry did not like this, so Jerome made enemies as well as friends and was forced to leave the city. Some wealthy women of Rome, who believed in his teaching, followed Jerome to Bethlehem, where they built convents for the women and a monastery for the men.

Among the Judean hills, looking out over the land where so much had happened, Jerome began to translate the Bible into Latin. The Old Testament had been written in Hebrew and the New Testament in Greek, but by this time people spoke Latin in the Church.

Some of the nuns helped Jerome with his work of translating the Bible. Their quiet life gave them time to study. Both nuns and monks taught the children, cared for the sick, and were helpful in every way to the people of the town. When barbarian soldiers took Rome, and the people fled in all directions, many refugees found safety with Jerome and his monks in Bethlehem.

Meanwhile another Christian leader was in trouble because of the difference between his beliefs and those of an empress.

In Milan, Italy, a sound of singing echoed through the streets. It came from a church, and the church was surrounded by soldiers. Peering out of their windows, or watching from other safe places, people said wonderingly: "Do they not know that the empress has sent these soldiers to take possession of the church? What can they do but give it up?"

Well, they could sing. That's what Bishop Ambrose thought. And sing they did, while the soldiers shuffled their feet and waited for orders from the empress. They didn't know what to do when the bishop of Milan and his congregation shut themselves inside a church and wouldn't stop singing. The empress was puzzled too, for she could not make up her mind to order her soldiers to attack a church full of singing Christians. At last she sent word for the soldiers to return to the palace.

"Ambrose has won! Ambrose has won!" people said to each other joyfully. Ambrose was very popular. He had become bishop because the people demanded it, and would have no other.

Ambrose brought more music into the worship of the Church. He wrote hymns and chants, and taught his congregation to sing them. Some of his hymns are in our hymnbook today.

There was a man named Augustine in the church on the day when Ambrose defied the empress and her soldiers. He had come from his home in North Africa to be a teacher in Milan. He was not yet a Christian, but he admired Ambrose and went to hear him preach.

It was not easy for Augustine to decide to become a Christian. As a boy and as a young man he had done many things he was later ashamed of. Sometimes Augustine loved pleasure above all else; sometimes he was more eager to find what was true and good. Augustine caused his parents a great deal of trouble until he was old enough to go to the university. Then he gave up his wild companions and studied hard to win honors.

After hearing Ambrose preach in Milan, Augustine began to read the Bible carefully, but there were still times when he wanted to do things he knew were not right. One day a friend from Africa told him about the monks and their life in the monasteries. Augustine felt ashamed that these simple men could live such hard, self-sacrificing lives while he was not able to control his own actions. He went out into a garden to think. There he heard a child's voice saying, "Take up and read." Augustine picked up a New Testament and opened it. As he read, he felt all the doubts and conflicts that had troubled him melt away. He felt sure he could now overcome his temptations, with Christ's help, and he was baptized by Bishop Ambrose on the following Easter eve. After a while Augustine went back to his home in North Africa and became bishop of Hippo.

And now, like a storm which has rumbled and threatened to break for a long time, the barbarian conquerors swept over the Roman Empire. When Alaric, the leader of the Goths, came to the walls of Rome, the emperor had fled from the city. Only the

bishop of Rome was left to meet the enemy.

The refugees from Rome, who had lost all they possessed, wanted to blame someone for their trouble. Many were not Christians, and they began to say the same things that had been said before. "Rome was strong," they said, "when we worshiped the gods of our fathers. Now see what Christianity has done to the Empire!"

Even the Christians were distressed, for they too had been forced to leave their homes. "Why is God punishing his people this way?" they asked themselves.

The answer came from Augustine, bishop of Hippo. "Empires rise and fall," Augustine said, "but the Church lives on forever. We need not be afraid if Rome dies, so long as the Church goes on. The Church is the City of God, not Rome!" Augustine wrote a great book called *The City of God*. In it he answered most of the questions that were worrying people. The writings and teachings of Augustine did much to keep Christianity alive in Europe during those dark and terrible days. In one of his books we find this lovely prayer: "Thou hast made us for Thyself and our hearts are restless till they find their rest in Thee."

Army after army of warriors from the north came down upon the Roman world. Augustine's own cathedral city of Hippo was starved and looted by the Vandals, but he did not live to see this. Later, on the road north of Rome, a strange meeting took place. Attila, leader of the Huns, a fierce tribe from Central Asia, came sweeping into Italy through the mountain passes to threaten Rome. Facing the Hun warrior stood an old man in full ceremonial robes—Leo, bishop of Rome. Leo had come to command Attila to spare his city.

Attila or any of his men could have struck Leo down with one swing of the sword, but they were too much surprised. The fierce Attila had never before

seen a man who was not afraid of him! He took a large ransom from Rome, but he did not loot or destroy the city. Two years later, another army of barbarians did that.

So the Roman Empire in western Europe came crashing to the dust under the heel of the conquering tribes of the north. But out of it arose a new kind of power which was to conquer the conquerors. The Christian Church, Augustine's City of God, would live on.

"How did the Church conquer the barbarian tribes when Rome couldn't?" asked Michael.

"By teaching them the Gospel of Christ," answered Mr. Wells. "And don't think for a minute that didn't take more courage than any other kind of warfare."

"It was the kind of warfare Paul meant," said Father, "when he told his friends to 'take the shield of faith, and the helmet of salvation, and the sword of the Spirit, which is the word of God.'"

"I guess it did take braver men to fight with weapons like that," said Michael. "Anyhow, the Church won."

"Next time," said Mr. Wells, "we'll see how they did it."

6. The Church Conquers the Conquerors

"How sweet the peonies smell!" Mother looked at the bushes bordering the path. "They'll be lovely for Children's Day next Sunday."

"It seems funny to have Children's Day in the assembly room of the school," said Joan.

Mr. Wells smiled. "Perhaps we'll be in the new church next year. Hello! Here come the others."

Michael and Don flung themselves down beside Mr. Wells's chair.

"You said you would tell us what happened after Rome fell," Michael reminded him.

"It was quite a different scene from this quiet garden," Mr. Wells began.

THE Roman Empire lay helpless as fierce tribes from the north swarmed over Europe. Rome's palaces and churches had been stripped of their treasures, and many buildings were in ruins. Terror and confusion were everywhere.

To whom could people turn in this dark hour? There was only one hope, the Church of Christ. It stood like a rock to protect and lead its suffering people, whose hearts cried out to God for peace and safety. The people looked to the bishop of Rome as to a father. They even gave him the title "pope,"

which comes from the Greek word meaning "father."
Because he was the only strong leader left, the pope
became the head of all the Christian churches.

After Rome fell, the Church not only held its own
people together, but also made plans to win the barbarian kingdoms. In this the popes were helped by
the monks, who traveled on foot over many miles of
broken Roman roads to carry the Christian message
to faraway places. The monks had changed many of
their ideas since the days when they fled to the
Egyptian desert. Benedict, a monk of Italy, had
built a monastery which was the first of many called
by his name. Benedict's rules for the monks were
strict but sensible. The old rules of being unmarried,

poor, and obedient were still the same, but Benedict expected more and more time to be given to work and study, prayer and service.

In Rome a monk named Gregory knelt in prayer, asking God to show him how he might help the people of his city. Gregory had been the mayor of Rome. When he could not prevent the terrible things that were happening, he threw aside his robes of office and became a Benedictine monk. "There is no salvation for my people but in God!" he cried.

Gregory had seen many sad sights in the Roman slave market, where human beings were bought and sold. One morning he noticed a little group of boys who looked different from the dark-skinned and black-haired people around them. These boys had blue eyes and fair skin. Their hair was like gold. "Where do they come from?" asked Gregory.

"From the far north," he was told. "From the province of Britain. The boys are Angles."

"They look like angels," said Gregory. "I will have them taught in the monastery school and send them back to teach their people in Angle-land."

Then Gregory became pope and had plenty to do, bringing order back to the ruined city of Rome. He rebuilt the churches which had been destroyed, and made their worship more beautiful. Many chants used in the Church were called by his name.

But Gregory did not forget the red-cheeked boys from Angle-land. He wanted to win this far corner of the north, not with the sword but with the message of Christ and his Church. Six years later he sent the abbot of his monastery to do this work.

It took Augustine and the forty monks who went with him six months to reach Britain. The tales they heard of the fierce pagans who lived there nearly turned them back in the first days of their journey. Indeed Augustine did go back to ask Gregory if it would not be better to forget these barbarous Angles. But Gregory said the monks must finish what they had started to do. So the little company went off on their long journey. Often their feet were blistered and their robes caked with dust, but they kept on.

Sometimes, as they made their way through a woodland or along the ridge of a mountain, the sound of chanting reached their tired ears. Then the trees would open into a clearing where a low, thick-walled monastery stood. How gladly they trooped into this restful place, and how kindly the weary travelers were greeted! The monks of Benedict's order had built these places of refuge all over western Europe. They chopped down trees. cleared the land, and planted crops for their own needs and those of the people who came to them for shelter. These monasteries were also storehouses for treasures of Roman art and learning, saved when the barbarians looted the cities. In their cells the monks copied precious manuscripts so they should not be lost. The monasteries took the place of schools and colleges when there was no other means of education.

At last Augustine and his monks reached Britain. Lifting high a cross and a large picture of Christ, they marched into the town of Canterbury, singing the chants of the Church. Much to their surprise, the people were not the fierce pagans they had been led to expect. The Saxon king, who ruled at Canterbury, had married a Christian princess, so Augustine preached in a little stone chapel, built in Roman days, and there he baptized the king and his court.

Augustine and his monks were not the first Christian missionaries to Britain. But the early Christians there had been driven into the western moun-

tains by the Angles and Saxons, pirate bands from northern Europe who took possession of Britain. These little bands of Christians were often attacked by raiders from Ireland.

In one of these raids a boy named Patrick was kidnaped and carried off to Ireland, where he was forced to herd pigs for six years. He finally escaped to France, where he studied in a monastery to become a priest. One night, as he lay sleeping, a messenger seemed to stand beside him with letters from Ireland. "Come and teach Christ to the Irish children," the letters begged. Patrick could not refuse this plea, so he went back to the land that had once made him a slave. Here he worked and preached for many years. Later these Irish missionaries went into Scotland and from Scotland into England. There they met Augustine and his Roman monks, who were working up from the south. They did not always agree, for the Irish monks and British Christians were satisfied with their own way of doing things. They didn't want to be told that they must follow the rules of the Roman Church.

"I suppose they thought their own Church laws and customs were just as good," said Michael.

"Yes," said Don, "I can see why they didn't want to be governed by a pope who was way off in Rome. Some of them probably hadn't even heard of him."

Some of the differences between the monks were really not at all important. One dispute was about the right way to shave their heads! A more serious difference was the date on which the Irish celebrated Easter. Their calendar was an old one and did not follow the more scientific method used by the Romans in fixing the Easter date. This meant that two Easter dates were celebrated. The disagreements were settled at last, but it took a long time.

Near the time when Gregory the Great died, a camel driver in faraway Arabia was thinking about the God of the Jews and Christians. His name was Mohammed, and he lived in Mecca, the holy city of Arabia.

As Mohammed led his caravan over the sandy trails of the Arabian desert, he met and talked to other travelers. Many were Jews or Christians. "They are right about the one true God," said Mohammed. "Abraham was the first of his prophets and Jesus Christ was a true prophet. But now I am the prophet of God whom all men should follow."

When Mohammed began to preach in Mecca, the people laughed at him. Then, as he kept on preaching, they grew angry. At last Mohammed had to go to another city, where he soon won many followers. The Moslems, as they were called, became so strong that in a few years Mohammed was able to capture Mecca and destroy all its idols. Most of the people of Arabia accepted Mohammed as their prophet.

"We will now conquer the world for the only God, whose name is Allah!" cried Mohammed. But Mohammed died before he could carry out this plan. Other leaders, who followed him, led the Moslem armies into religious wars that lasted for a hundred years. Like a flame they fanned out both east and west. Within five years Jerusalem had fallen, and a few years later the great city of Alexandria and all of Egypt were in the hands of the Moslems.

On they went across North Africa, until they came to the Straits of Gibraltar. Crossing that narrow passage, they entered Spain and poured through the mountain passes into France. Here they were brought to a halt, one hundred years after Mohammed's death, by Charles Martel, ruler of the Franks. He won a great battle and pushed the followers of Mohammed back into Spain. The Christian world in Europe was saved.

By this time the differences between the Church of Rome and the English Church had been overcome. Pope Gregory II sent a young missionary from England to the Saxons in Germany. He called the young man Boniface, a Latin name meaning "Welldoer." One day as Boniface walked along a trail deep

in the forest, he came to a giant oak tree where pagan priests were offering sacrifices to their god Wotan. "I will show you that Wotan is not a god by cutting down this tree," said Boniface, picking up an ax. In spite of the fury of the priests, Boniface started to chop at the tree. As stroke after stroke cut deeper, a sudden wind swept through the branches and the great tree crashed to the ground. Its trunk split into four pieces. The Germans were now ready to listen when Boniface told them about the Christian God. They even helped him to build a Christian chapel from the wood of the sacred oak.

Charlemagne, king of the Franks, at last conquered the Saxons and forced them to become Christians. This was not the way Boniface would have chosen, and it did not make the best kind of Christians. Charlemagne was a great warrior and also a friend of the Church. A new empire was being built in which the emperor should have power to rule men on earth, and the pope should speak for God through the Church. On Christmas Day, in the year 800, Charlemagne knelt before the tomb of Saint Peter in the great church at Rome. There the pope placed a crown on Charlemagne's head and proclaimed him the "Holy Roman Emperor." "Now indeed," said Charlemagne proudly, "the City of God about which Augustine dreamed has come true. All Christians are united in a Kingdom of God, and I am its ruler on earth."

But, as time went by, the emperors, kings, and popes quarreled because each one was looking out for his own selfish gain. The people wanted to be loyal to the king, and also to be faithful to the pope as head of the Church. They did not know which side to take.

One winter day, long after Charlemagne's death, Henry, emperor of Germany, went climbing painfully up the icy slopes of the Alps. He was on his way to make his peace with Pope Gregory VII, who had put him out of the Church. The people were solidly behind the pope. Henry *might* lose his throne.

Hearing that Henry was crossing the mountains to meet him, the pope waited at a fortress called Canossa. He did not know whether Henry was coming with an army or not, so he chose a safe place. But Henry was wearing the white robe of a penitent, and he was very humble. Some of his men and horses had plunged to their death down the icy cliffs, and he wished only to finish this terrible trip. When he arrived, he went barefoot in the snow to the castle gate, but it was three days before the pope would see him.

As the gates swung open Henry was ready to do anything for a pardon. He forgot these promises after he went home, and a year later was put out of the Church again. This time he marched to Italy with his armies, and the pope hid in a fortress. Henry chose another pope, and Gregory VII died in exile.

"I like the story of the boys from Angle-land," said Joan.

"It seems funny," laughed Ann, "to think of missionaries going to England."

"And to France and Germany," added Don.

"The popes and the Roman emperors didn't always act like Christians themselves!" said Michael.

"That's true," said Mr. Wells. "While the Church had been making Christians of the barbarians, faults had been growing up like weeds within the Church itself. Pride, love of power, envy, and greed would still have to be overcome."

7. The Christian World Loses and Gains

Thunder rumbled overhead and long needles of rain were slashing at the garden. "I guess we'll have to stay indoors tonight," said Joan.

"We'll make it bright and cheerful here." Father touched a match to the log in the fireplace.

"This would be a good evening to buckle on our armor and start on a great adventure," said Mr. Wells.

"Where are we going?" Joan whirled around at this exciting idea.

"To the Holy Land," Mr. Wells answered. "The Christian world has made up its mind to win back from the Moslems the sacred places where Jesus lived and died."

"The Crusades!" cried Michael.

For two hundred years the green fields of France and the pleasant valleys of the Rhineland were shaken with the tread of marching feet. Armies streamed along roads leading to the East—strange armies with crosses sewed to their sleeves, and banners bearing the same sign. Kings and knights and nobles in armor clanked across drawbridges and rode away from their castles. Their horses' hoofs made the earth tremble as they thundered across Europe. Peasants left their farming and craftsmen their tools to form another kind of army. Without horses or armor, they set out toward the eastern lands from which many of them would never return.

Ever since the Turks, a warlike people of Asia, had taken Jerusalem, pilgrims had been coming home with tales of cruel treatment. Now the Turks were also trying to capture Constantinople. The emperor there had sent a messenger to the pope at Rome asking for help. Pope Urban proclaimed a religious war, or crusade, against the Turks. "All who join the Crusades," said the pope, "will be forgiven for their sins. Those who die will have eternal life."

A monk called Peter the Hermit went from town to town rousing great masses of people to wild excitement. Barefoot, and wearing only a coarse tunic, Peter carried an enormous cross and pleaded with the crowds not to leave the holy tomb of Christ in the hands of unbelievers. "They have been cruel to our pilgrims!" he cried. "Are you not ashamed to do nothing about it? Follow me to Jerusalem! God wills it!" And the cry echoed across the land: "God wills it!" Follow him they did, crowds and crowds of people who had no training and no weapons. But in Asia Minor the Turks were ready for them, and it did not take them long to destroy this untrained band.

The knights and nobles had spent the winter sharpening their swords and having their shields and armor hammered into shape by blacksmiths, so were well prepared. It took three years for their army to reach the walls of Jerusalem. When at last the Crusaders

saw the Holy City, they fell on their knees and thanked God. But Jerusalem stood high on three hills, and it was protected by thick walls. It took a month to scale those walls and beat back the Moslems. Then, sad to say, the Crusaders fell upon the people of Jerusalem with their swords, and put them to death. Afterward they marched to the Church of the Holy Sepulchre to give thanks for their victory.

"I don't believe God thought much of that prayer," said Michael.

"It certainly wasn't Jesus' kind of prayer," agreed Ann.

The Crusaders held Jerusalem nearly a hundred years. Then a great Moslem leader recaptured the city. Kings of Germany, France, and England led other crusades to try to win it back and many lives and fortunes were lost. Whole armies sometimes perished before they came anywhere near Palestine.

Even children caught the crusading fever. Stephen, a boy of France, thought he had seen a vision of Christ telling him that the children could do what the older people could not. "Christ," said Stephen, "will help us. He will make the waters of the sea open as God did for Moses and the people of Israel. We will not conquer with swords, but in the power of the Lord Jesus." Boys and girls left their homes and raced off to join others who were gathering in towns and villages. Nothing could hold them back. In Germany another boy, named Nicholas, heard the news. Thousands strong, the German children marched away up the Rhine valley toward the snowy peaks of the Swiss Alps, while the French children marched south to Marseilles. Young voices shouted, "God wills it!" or sang as they marched along.

But by and by their voices grew fainter. Some were lost in the forests or among the icy peaks of the Alps. Those who reached Rome were persuaded by the pope to go back to their homes. Other children, who had followed Stephen to the shores of the Mediterranean Sea, found that the waters did not roll back for them. Some traders offered to take them to Palestine in their boats, but these boys and girls never saw the Holy Land. All who were not shipwrecked were sold by the traders as slaves in Egypt. This is one of the saddest stories told of the Crusades.

Two hundred years is a long time. The first Crusaders came home or were buried in a foreign land,

and their sons and grandsons followed them. Kings and emperors, bishops and popes died. The returning Crusaders were not the same men who had marched away to the East. They had seen great Eastern cities, and people whose ways of life were very different from their own. They came back with new ideas.

Many a noble and knight looked up as he approached the harsh gray walls of his castle and thought of the gay island city of Venice, with its colorful palaces and blue lagoons; or the golden domes of Constantinople; or the rich bazaars of Antioch and Damascus. He thought how pleased his wife and daughters would be when he gave them the damask cloth which he had brought home, and the royal purple dyes from Tyre. He would show them how to use powder and perfume, like Eastern women. He would make their eyes sparkle with a glimpse of themselves in a little glass mirror, such as they had never before seen. There was a rug, too, with rich Oriental color that would brighten the smoke-darkened timbers of the great hall of the castle.

But it was not alone the new things brought back by the Crusaders that changed Europe. They had discovered the best ways to travel between West and East. Merchants from Asia and Africa could now find markets for their goods in Europe. New towns were built where trade flourished. In them the gold of merchants, the skill of craftsmen, and the labor of men, women, and children were used to create glorious churches. They were called the Gothic cathedrals.

"Why don't *you* tell us about the cathedrals?" Mr. Wells asked Father. "You know how they were built better than I do."

"I don't believe I'm quite the storyteller you are," said Father, "but I'll try."

After a moment's thought, he began:

Long lines of people wound up the slope of a hill overlooking the farmlands of the Eure River valley in France. They climbed slowly, for they were harnessed to carts piled high with wood and stone or other building materials. Some were pulling wagons full of corn. Even the children pulled small carts. Every person from the town of Chartres and for miles around, rich and poor alike, was bringing whatever he had to offer toward the building of a new church.

The blackened wall was all that remained of their church of "Our Lady" which had been three times destroyed by fire. There the people of Chartres unloaded their carts. Noblewomen took off their jewels and heaped them in baskets. All who had money offered it gladly, and those who had only strong arms and backs, gave their labor. Peasants who had farms brought their crops to feed the workers. The children who helped that day were sixty years old before the full glory of Notre Dame of Chartres overshadowed their homes.

These children watched stone placed upon stone, and saw the walls rise until they were a gray mist in the soaring arches overhead. They saw, as the years went by, armies of craftsmen and artists working inside and out. Cold stone was carved into decorations that were like frozen lace. Lifelike figures, set in niches or over the great doorways, told the history and teaching of the Church better than words.

The children peered into the sheds where glassmakers were creating stained glass, and later watched while panes of glowing crimsons, blues, and purples were fitted into the stone arches which framed the windows. They gazed in wonder at the light pouring through a great rose window, as brilliant as precious stones. There would be nearly two hundred of these windows. In them people would learn to read the story of their faith pictured in little scenes from the Bible or in the faces of Christian saints and martyrs.

"Now it's your turn," said Father to Mr. Wells. So Mr. Wells took up the story.

All the time the Church at Rome was getting richer and more powerful. The pope was really the ruler of Europe. He gave kingdoms and took them away whenever it suited him. "I am the successor of Saint Peter," declared the pope, "and what I say or do is for the highest good of everyone."

Sometimes people did not agree with him, especially kings and emperors who were apt to have plans of their own. But if the pope refused them the sacraments of the Church and put their countries under a ban, it would mean that church services could not be held anywhere. The Church was too important in the life of the people for this to be allowed to happen. The people believed that the pope spoke for God and that their first duty was to obey him. So kings and emperors usually had to give in.

About this time a young man in the Italian town of Assisi began to think that riches were causing all the trouble in the world. Men fought for land and money. Even the monasteries had grown rich, and the monks did not work so hard to help the poor. "I will give up my riches and live the life of the poor," decided this young man, whose name was Francis. He put on a rough brown robe, tied around the waist with a piece of rope. He would share the life of the poor, and bring them help and comfort and the love of Christ.

Francis called himself a "brother," and it was not long before Brother Francis was known and loved all through the countryside. Brother Francis loved all small creatures, and often answered birdcalls with a soft whistle that would bring the birds with a flurry of wings to perch on his shoulders. He called them his brothers and sisters, and he never failed to thank God for them or for all the other wonderful things God had made. Other men followed his example when they saw how happy he was in this life of service and poverty, and what joy he brought to all kinds of people. The only rule that Francis required of his followers was that they should try to live like Jesus and obey the commands that he had given to his disciples. Pope Innocent III gave his approval to this little band of brothers, calling them the Franciscans. They never had a monastery but within a few years there were thousands of these good brothers carrying on their work for Christ in many lands.

It is at Christmastide that we think especially of Brother Francis, for it was he who gave us the lovely custom of making the Christmas crèche. He wanted to soften the hearts of people who were not very kind or very good by letting them see the beautiful story of the birth of Jesus as though it were happening before their eyes. In a cave on the side of a hill, Brother Francis and his helpers built a manger and filled it with hay. Then they brought a real ox and ass and tied them near the manger. Finally a living baby

was laid in the manger. When people crowded inside the cave, they gazed in surprise and then dropped to their knees, for it made them remember how God had sent his Son to earth in just such a humble place. Their hearts were filled with love for the Child of Bethlehem, and all the meanness and unkindness seemed to melt away.

"I have a picture of Saint Francis preaching a sermon to the birds," said Ann.

"Many such stories are told about him," said Mr. Wells. "Often his pulpit was in the open fields, with the sky for a roof."

"That was a different kind of church from the big cathedrals Father has been telling us about," said Michael.

"Both were for the praise of God," said Father, "so they were not so very different after all."

"I'm glad we won't be sixty years old before our church is finished—like the children at Chartres," said Joan.

8. Western Europe Wakes Up and Asks Questions

"Don and I watched the men working on the new church this afternoon," said Michael, as the last crumb of a picnic supper on the lawn had been eaten. "Trucks were dumping sand and gravel."

"We were thinking," added Don, "how much slower it would be if we had to drag our own loads of wood and stone—like the people who built the cathedrals."

"We can all work together as they did," said Mr. Wells, "even if not in just the same way."

"In those days all the people in the town went to one big church. Why do we have so many different kinds of churches today?" asked Joan.

"Because a time came when people began to ask questions," Mr. Wells answered.

For a long time the people of western Europe had been willing to do and think whatever they were told by the emperor and pope, but now they started to think for themselves. Some had learned to read the Bible and they found that the teaching of Jesus did not agree with what the bishops and priests of the Church told them. People were losing faith in leaders so many of whom were guilty of greediness, love of luxury, anger, and pride.

The first Crusaders who came back from the East

were tired of war and sick at heart because of the cruel things they had seen done in the name of Christ. They found it was almost as bad at home. Church leaders were busy with their own selfish plans. Thousands of people in the rapidly growing towns lived in misery and fear. Some of the returning Crusaders felt so discouraged that they made up their minds that the world was altogether evil. With others who felt the same way, they began to separate themselves from the Church and form groups of their own. They chose their own ministers and worshiped in their own way. The Church of Rome called this heresy, which means thinking the wrong way. "I must stamp out all these heresies," said Pope Innocent III. "They are springing up in too many places."

First he tried sending Dominican brothers to win back those who had wandered from the Church. Like the Franciscans, they followed a life of poverty and sacrifice, and might in time have won the heretics by their preaching and example, but Pope Innocent couldn't wait for that. He and his successors destroyed or scattered them in a struggle that went on many years. But still people did not stop thinking for themselves. Many were going to school and learning to read the works of famous writers. Knowledge was changing the way people thought about the world, and it also made them ask questions about the teaching of the Church.

A scholar named Thomas Aquinas bent over his

desk and wrote slowly with a long goose-quill pen. He was writing a book that would tell plainly just what the Church believed and taught. People were no longer satisfied to be told, "This is so." They were asking, "Why?" So Aquinas' goose-quill pen scratched along, putting down in careful Latin the Church's answers to the questions men were asking.

And what were some of these questions? "What is God like?" "How may we know him better?" "Who is man?" "Where did he come from and why is he here?" "Where is he going?" "What is God's will for man?"

"God shows us what he is like," answered Aquinas, "through the things he has created—the world and man himself. But that is not all. God speaks through the Bible, which the Church explains and teaches. The best way to understand God is to know Jesus Christ. God gave man his life, and man is here to do God's will by practicing faith, hope, and love." Thomas Aquinas spent nine years writing this great book, and died before it was finished.

Meanwhile the people of the British Isles were also asking questions. For three hundred years England had been growing into a nation, and the people had come to dislike taking orders from Rome. They had seen false beliefs and evil customs creeping into the Church of Rome. They were no longer willing to obey the pope as head of all the churches.

During this time a child was born in a little English village who grew up to become one of the most popular teachers at Oxford University. This man, named John Wyclif, was saying: "If you want answers to your questions, go to the Bible. It is the Word of God, and has the only true answers. Christ will show you the way, but it is a way of humility, love, and poverty."

Wyclif preached against the false teaching of the Church. Church leaders were very angry. The pope at Rome ordered Wyclif's arrest, and a church council condemned him for heresy. Wyclif could no longer teach at Oxford, but he continued to work among the poor and preach at his little church in the country. He repeated over and over again: "The Church is not the pope and cardinals; it is the whole company of Christian people, whose Head is Christ. The Church is you—and you—and you, if you follow the law of the Scriptures."

But how could uneducated people read the Bible when it was written in Latin? Wyclif got some of his friends to help him, and they began to translate the Bible into English. When it was finished, this Bible in their own tongue was a great wonder to the people. As there was no printing press at this time, copies had to be written by hand. It took nearly a year to make one copy, so the cost was about two hundred dollars—a year's wages. People who could not afford a whole Bible were willing to trade a load of hay for just a few pages of their own, or for the privilege of sharing a neighbor's copy for an hour each day. Some even learned parts of the Bible by heart and recited them for those who could not have the written page.

And now, over the green hills and through the pleasant valleys of England, the "poor priests," or Lollards, sent out by Wyclif, carried the Gospel to little towns and villages. They often stopped at the door of a tiny thatch-roofed cottage to ask for a cup of milk or a piece of bread. Like the early disciples, they carried nothing with them except the precious manuscripts which would make the Bible known in the homes of the countryfolk of England. Old people,

leaning over their peat fire, or a farmer and his wife, with their children around them, listened in wonder. Here were words they could understand!

Many were arrested and some were burned for heresy, for the Roman Church did not want the Bible in the hands of the people. But all over England copies of the Bible were secretly read and studied.

In Bohemia, John Hus was carrying on Wyclif's teaching. He was a fiery preacher and was bound to bring punishment upon himself. A great Church council was held in Switzerland. There Hus was asked to come and explain his teachings to the pope, the emperor, and hundreds of other churchmen.

Although they had promised him that he could come and go in safety, Hus was accused of heresy and imprisoned. At his trial he was asked, "Will you take back what you have taught?" Hus answered, "Some of the things you accuse me of I have never taught." "Will you take them back anyway?" persisted his judges. "No!" said Hus. So the council condemned him to be burned. Because of this cruelty, Hus's followers started a war which lasted many years.

Some people showed this feeling of rebellion in a different way. Quiet groups of men, women, and children lived together in a community of loving fellowship like the first Christians. They did not make war, and they built no churches or monasteries of their own. They only tried to make the spirit of Jesus Christ speak through their lives.

In Germany a way had been found to copy books by setting little letters of soft lead in wooden presses. Whole pages of manuscript could be printed at one time. The Bible was the first book to be printed. In England, William Tyndale was able to print in English the New Testament that John Wyclif had copied by hand one hundred and fifty years before.

The Church had spies everywhere, looking for those who disobeyed its laws. Tyndale had to go to Germany to do his work, but even there he was discovered, and hundreds of copies of his New Testament were burned on the printing presses.

That was not all. One day in London, people went running to the square near Old Saint Paul's Cathedral,

where a great bonfire had been lighted. Thousands of copies of Tyndale's New Testament had been shipped to England, hidden in bales of linen or sacks of flour. Now, they too were being burned. But Tyndale never gave up. "In burning the book, they did none other than I looked for," he said, "and no more shall they do if they burn me also."

This did indeed happen. But before he died Tyndale got a large number of his New Testaments into England. By this time something else had happened which priests and bishops, cardinals and popes could not stop. It began when a German monk wrote his ideas on a piece of parchment and nailed it to the door of a church.

"He must have thought his ideas were pretty important," said Michael.

"But why did he nail the parchment on a church door?" asked Joan.

"The church door was a kind of bulletin board," answered Mr. Wells, "and an invitation to discuss ideas with other people."

"What was on the paper?" Michael asked.

"Ninety-five reasons why he thought the Church was teaching and doing many things that were wrong."

"Did he get into trouble?" asked Don.

"Lots of trouble," said Mr. Wells. "But that is another story."

9. New Voices and New Ideas

"Here they come—Mr. Wells and all the rest!" Michael called through the window. Joan ran out to the garden.

"What did they do to Martin Luther?" asked Don, when they were all seated.

"Suppose we start at the beginning, when Martin Luther was a boy singing in the streets of a German town," said Mr. Wells.

Young Martin Luther was thin and pale, but he put his whole heart into his singing, for this was the way he earned his living. His bright eyes watched the passers-by. *Will someone*, he wondered, *help pay for my supper?* Martin was the son of a miner who had very little money, but was anxious for him to go to school. In those days a student often paid for his schooling by begging on the streets. Martin had a sweet voice, so he sang on the street and also in church choirs.

One day a woman stopped to listen to his singing. She did more than hand him money; she and her husband offered Martin a home. Now that he had a comfortable place to live and food to eat, Martin could study better. His high marks in school pleased his new friends as well as his parents. "You shall be a lawyer," Hans Luther said to his son. But Martin Luther disappointed his parents by becoming a monk.

"Why do you want to go into a monastery?" his friends asked him. "Don't you know how greedy and lazy the monks have grown? The Church is taking most of our money in taxes to spend in Rome."

"Yes, I know all that," answered Martin, "but *I* shall try to be a good monk. I want to spend my life in study, and in prayer that God will save me from my sins."

Martin Luther had grown up with fear of God in his heart. The Church taught that God would punish people when they died, unless they obeyed the rules laid down for them by the priests. In the monastery he almost killed himself by fasting and praying for hours at a time. Still he did not find peace or happiness.

One day, after he had become a teacher, Luther sat reading Paul's letter to the Romans. "The righteous shall live by faith," Paul had written. *What does that mean?* Luther wondered. *It must mean that people can never make up for their sinfulness by torturing themselves or by doing good deeds. They must hear the good news that God forgives their sins freely and gives them peace.*

Of course this was different from the Church's teaching. According to the Church, forgiveness for sins was in the hands of the priests. The main thing was to do what the priest ordered. Luther had seen pilgrims in Rome climbing the long sacred stairways on their knees so that the pope would give them a letter of pardon, called an "indulgence." He had seen people paying money to priests for such indulgences, which they thought would protect them no matter how often they did wrong.

About this time a Dominican brother was selling indulgences to raise money for St. Peter's Church in Rome. He frightened the peasants into buying them with tales of terrible punishment. "You can also help

your relatives and friends who have died to get to heaven," he told them. "All you need to do is to drop your coins in my box."

"This is wicked and must be stopped!" said Luther. "The Church is wrong to let dishonest priests stir up the fears of people and take their money for a promise of forgiveness that means nothing. The priests are leading them in the wrong way."

On All Saints' Day, when the people of Wittenberg were crowding into the church, they saw a long piece of parchment nailed to the door. "What does it say? Who wrote it?" they asked one another.

"It says that any Christian who repents of his sins will receive God's forgiveness without buying a pardon from the priests!" shouted a man who was standing close enough to read the words.

Soon all the people were pushing and craning their necks to see what else was written, and whose name was signed to these startling statements. Everybody knew who Martin Luther was, and his words were worth thinking about. But Luther had no idea that his opinions would spread over the country like wildfire.

Luther began to preach that Christians should follow what was written in the Bible. "The pope," he said, "is not the only person who can say what the Scriptures mean. You can find out for yourselves if you read the Bible. The rules for Christian living are written there plainly."

The pope and his cardinals in Rome were worried about what was happening in the north. "Who," they asked, "is this Martin Luther? He thinks he knows what is right while everything the Church has been teaching for more than a thousand years is wrong. He must come to Rome and explain what he means."

But Martin Luther did not go to Rome. He knew too well what would happen if he did. When the pope ordered him put out of the Church and his books burned, Luther called the people of Wittenberg together and had a bonfire of his own. He threw the pope's order in the flames, while everyone sang and cheered. "All Germany must stand together against Rome," said Luther.

The pope was now very angry. "Anyone with ideas like this German monk must be punished severely," he declared. The emperor, Charles V, who was head of both Church and State, was holding an important meeting about that time. All the princes and nobles of Germany and all the cardinals and archbishops of the Church were to be there. Luther was commanded to come and defend himself before this gathering.

Would he go? "No," said his friends, "it would mean his death."

"Yes," said Luther, "I will go, even though there are as many devils as there are tiles on the roofs."

But Martin Luther had every reason to be afraid, when he looked into the cold faces of the men waiting for him to speak. They would judge him without mercy, and nothing he could say would make any difference, unless he took back everything he had said or written. Luther stood in his black monk's gown before the throne of the emperor with its golden canopy. Cardinals in scarlet robes and richly dressed nobles leaned forward in the glare of the torches which lighted the great hall. The old town seemed to hold its breath as Martin Luther spoke.

"Unless you can show me by the Bible that I am wrong," he said, "I will not take back anything. The Word of God is my guide."

Some of the German princes were on Luther's side, so the emperor gave him a day to think it over. Then Luther was asked: "Do you take back your teaching? Answer, 'Yes,' or, 'No.'"

"I cannot deny what I believe. God help me!"

answered Luther clearly, so that all could hear.

The emperor had promised that Luther should go from the meeting in safety, but Luther's friends did not trust this promise. They sent men to seize him on the homeward journey and take him to a place where he was sure to be safe. Luther lived for nearly a year hidden away in the Castle of the Wartburg.

During this time Luther began to translate the New Testament into German. But after a while he decided to go back to Wittenberg even though it might mean being burned at the stake. Luckily for Luther, the emperor was fighting a war which would keep him away from Germany for a long time. Both the emperor and the pope were too busy to pay much attention to Luther, as they were quarreling over who should rule Italy. This gave Luther a good chance to work for the kind of Church he believed in, and soon Lutheran churches were increasing throughout Germany and other countries.

Luther finished translating the Bible into German, which even the poorer people could read and understand. Everyone hurried to buy copies as fast as they could be printed. Church services were also in the language of the people instead of Latin, and Bible-reading was an important part of the service. Luther loved music. Like Bishop Ambrose of Milan he taught his congregations to sing and he wrote many hymns.

Now that he was separated from the Roman Catholic Church, Luther felt that the vows he had taken to

become a monk were no longer binding. Many monks and nuns felt the same way, and they began to marry like other people. This ended monastery life. Luther married a former nun and they had five children, whom Luther loved very dearly. "According to the Scriptures," said Luther, "ministers and priests should be free to live like other Christians."

While he lived to see the Lutheran Church become strong in most of the German states, Luther did not have an easy time. The struggle with the Church of Rome went on, and Luther was under threat of death as long as he lived.

Meanwhile people in other countries were also working for a better Church. They were called Reformers, and later were known as Protestants.

In Zurich, Switzerland, a Reformer named Zwingli made still more changes in Church worship. "I find nothing in the Bible that commands us to have images or crosses or organs in the churches, so we will take them out," said Zwingli. People in some of the towns thought this meant that they could go around pulling down and smashing all the images they found in churches and other public places, and they destroyed many beautiful things.

Another group of Protestants in Zurich believed that every word of the Bible was law and that no other law should govern their Church. These people were called "Anabaptists," or sometimes "Baptists," because they thought only those who were ready to join the Church should be baptized. "The Bible," said the Baptists, "does not say to baptize babies. The apostles baptized people who were old enough to know whether they wanted to become Christians or not. Also, the first Christians had nothing to do with earthly rulers, so why should we?" The Baptists were treated very cruelly. Some met death by drowning and others were burned. Driven out of the churches, they wandered through Europe until they later found safety in Holland, Canada, and America.

Geneva, another city of Switzerland, became as important to the Protestants as Rome was to the Catholics. Geneva was a very old city, whose people had struggled for centuries to keep their freedom. When the Reformers started their work, Geneva was governed by both Protestants and Roman Catholics. William Farel, a Protestant minister, tried hard to form a city government that was all Protestant, and at last he succeeded. "Now," said Farel, "I must have someone to help me make Geneva grow into a strong Protestant center."

Just at this time, John Calvin, a French Reformer, came to Geneva to escape persecution. *Here is the man*, thought Farel, *who will know how to plan the new churches and schools we must have.* So he begged Calvin to stay in Geneva.

Walking through the hilly streets of the old city, Calvin could see the beauty of the country all around him. Perhaps he said to himself: "I will try to make

this city as beautiful for God as nature has made it for man. The faith preached here shall be as pure as the snow on that mountain peak, and it shall flow out into the world as the blue waters of Lake Geneva are carried into France."

It was not an easy task. France, a Roman Catholic country, was very close, and there was danger that her armies might capture Geneva at any time. French Protestants, the Huguenots, were being treated badly at home and were crowding into Geneva. People came also from Italy, Holland, Scotland, and England.

Calvin taught that the Bible was the Word of God, and that men must obey the will of God as it was written there. Life in Geneva followed a very strict plan. It was not enough for the refugees to say that they believed in the reformed faith; their actions must show it. "Unless you make your life as perfect as possible," said Calvin, "you cannot stay in Geneva."

From his pulpit in St. Peter's Cathedral, Calvin preached a Gospel that made people willing to face peril and suffering. They carried his teaching to all the countries of Europe, and later to the new world. No one thought of staying away from Church, although there were two services on Sunday and one at dawn three days of the week. Like Luther, Calvin believed in a singing congregation. His hymnbook was based on the psalms, which were the hymns of Jesus' day.

"Some of our hymns today are taken from the psalms," said Mother.

"I know one," cried Joan. "'The King of Love My Shepherd Is.' That's the Twenty-third Psalm."

"Yes, and there are many others. We'll look for them in our hymnal."

Calvin also wrote a lesson book with questions and answers about Christian teaching. It was called the Catechism, and every boy and girl, as well as the older people, had to study it. He planned a very fine school system, where even the youngest children were taught how to live as Christians. Calvin trained hundreds of Protestant leaders, who went back to their own countries to spread the reformed faith.

One of the men who studied under Calvin came from Scotland. His name was John Knox. He founded the Presbyterian Church of Scotland, and in it he taught many things that he had learned from Calvin.

"The Presbyterian Church is our Church too," Joan said, with an air of having suddenly found herself right in the midst of the story.

"Why was it called Presbyterian?" Michael asked.

"Because," answered Mr. Wells, "the word 'presbyter' is a Greek word meaning 'elder,' and Calvin planned his Church government to include a group of men, called elders, who should work with the minister for the good of the people."

"Where did my Church begin?" Ann wanted to know.

Mr. Wells smiled at Ann. "It started as the Church of England, and later became the Protestant Episcopal Church in America. We'll hear more about your Church next time."

10. Hard Days for the Protestants

"Here comes Janet!" cried Joan, jumping up and running to meet a girl who was coming across the lawn.

"Janet is my new friend," Joan explained to Mr. Wells, when they came back together. "She lives in Scotland, but she's here visiting her aunt. She calls her church a 'kirk.'"

Mr. Wells held out his hand. "We are going to talk about the 'kirk' of Scotland, Janet. Have you heard of John Knox?"

"Oh, yes! Every Scot has heard of John Knox. We have a statue of him in Edinburgh."

"Why? Was he a hero?" Michael asked.

"I'll tell you the story and you can decide for yourself," said Mr. Wells.

A FRENCH galley cut through the choppy waters of the North Sea. Fresh winds swelled her sails and sang in the rigging, while the men at the oars bent and pulled, bent and pulled—forward and backward, forward and backward—in time to the crack of a whip.

One of the rowers stole a quick glance at the shore line in the distance. Against the sky he could see the

spire of a church. "Yes," John Knox said to himself, "we are close to the coast of Scotland. There is the church where I used to preach." The muscles of his arms and back bulged as he tightened his grip on the oars and pulled hard. "I will go back," he muttered, "and I will preach and preach until the kirk of Scotland becomes Protestant!"

For many months Knox had been chained to his bench as a galley slave. The French had made him a prisoner for preaching the Protestant faith in Scotland. England was already Protestant, and France was determined that this should not happen in Scotland where the queen was a French princess.

At last the day came when Knox was set free, but it was not safe for him to go back to Scotland at once. Instead he went to England, which for a long time had been listening to the voices of the Reformers across the English Channel. From the days when John Wyclif's "poor priests" carried the handwritten English Bible from one end of the country to the other, the people of England had turned more and more to the Scriptures as their guide, and less to the Church of Rome. They were glad to listen when some of their ministers began to preach the new Protestant teaching which English students were bringing back from Germany and Switzerland. But it was King Henry VIII who had decided that England should become a Protestant nation. Henry wanted a son to follow him as king of England, but of his five children, only one girl was living. The only way he could have an heir was by marrying another wife. But the pope at Rome said, "No!" There was a Church law which forbade even a king to leave one wife for another.

England was now a strong and independent nation whose people did not like to be told what they could or could not do. "All right," said Henry, "I will separate the Church in England from the Church in Rome!" So there came to be a new Church called the Church of England.

Henry made very few changes at first, except to have English Bibles take the place of Latin ones. This was only a short time after Tyndale had been burned at the stake. Tyndale's last prayer had been, "Lord, open the king of England's eyes." His prayer was answered, for a year later copies of Tyndale's New Testament were being placed in all the churches. Henry was also planning for another translation of the whole Bible.

It was not until Henry's third marriage that the son he had wanted so much was born. When John Knox went to England after being released as a galley slave, Henry had died and his son Edward was king. Because the boy was only twelve years old, Edward's uncle was the real ruler. He was a Protestant and he made many more changes in the Church. Instead of Latin, the English language was used in worship. A collection of prayers and services called *The Book of Common Prayer* was put together. Most of the people liked these changes, and the Protestant Church grew stronger. But all this stopped when the young king died.

Edward's half sister Mary, who was a strong Roman Catholic, now came to the throne, and soon began to make the Protestants suffer. John Knox, with many other Protestants, fled to Geneva. Later he said that Geneva was "the most perfect school of Christ that ever was on the earth since the days of the apostles."

At last the time came when Knox could return to his own country. A Protestant queen, Elizabeth, was now reigning in England, and Knox hoped to make

Scotland Protestant also. He wanted to unite the two countries as one nation, but this did not happen at once. Knox's return and his fiery preaching stirred the people so much that they began to destroy Roman Catholic churches and monasteries. Mobs smashed images and stopped services. French soldiers were called in, and a struggle between the French and Scots followed which might have ended badly for the Reformers if the English queen had not helped them.

About this time a French ship sailed into a Scottish port bringing a new queen to Scotland. Mary Queen of Scots had been brought up a Roman Catholic, and she had no idea of listening to or following Protestant teaching. Neither had John Knox any thought of obeying a Catholic queen. "I shall soon make him understand that subjects must obey their queen," said Mary, and she tried at first to talk with him in a friendly way. "No," said Knox, "I will obey no queen who tries to destroy the Protestant Church, for it is the true Church." At last both Protestants and Catholics were against Mary, and she lost her throne. Later Knox's dream of seeing Scotland and England united came true. Queen Elizabeth died and the son of Mary Queen of Scots became king of both countries.

Meanwhile the Huguenots, Calvin's own countrymen, worked hard to reform the Church in France. Protestants and Catholics fought each other fiercely for many years, and neither side showed any mercy.

One summer night—the night of Saint Bartholomew
—thousands of Huguenots with their leaders were
killed. King Henry IV decided that there would be no
France left if these wars continued. He decreed that
France should be a Roman Catholic country, but
gave Protestants freedom to worship as they wished.
When, later, another French king took away this freedom, many of the Huguenots fled to England, Holland, and America.

About the time of the massacre of Saint Bartholomew, the powerful Roman Catholic ruler of Spain was
having trouble with Dutch subjects. "The Hollanders
pay me a good deal of money in taxes, which I badly
need," said Philip II of Spain, "but I cannot allow
them to be Protestants. How can I punish these
heretics without losing some of my income? If I burn
them at the stake they will pay no more taxes!"

Philip tried in a number of ways to get the Hollanders back into the Roman Catholic Church, but
nothing he said or threatened to do made much im-
pression. They went right on worshiping in their own
churches and listening to preachers who had been
trained by Luther, Zwingli, or Calvin. Philip was now
out of patience, so he sent his general, the duke of
Alva, to deal with these stubborn people. Alva started
right in executing the Protestant leaders. He attacked
Dutch cities and put thousands of innocent people to
death. But he met his match at the town of Leyden.

From May to October the citizens of Leyden had

defended their town against the besieging Spanish army and their food was almost gone. "They will have to surrender soon," gloated the Spanish soldiers. Then one morning a strange sight made Alva and his soldiers rub their eyes in amazement. Where dry land had been, they saw rippling water, over which flat barges and queer-looking boats of every kind were being rowed, pushed, or pulled toward the city walls. "They have cut the dikes and let in the sea!" gasped the Spaniards. "They are bringing relief to the city by water!" Leyden was saved, but the struggle went on for many years. In the end Holland became a strong Protestant country, with a Church much like the Presbyterian, which they called the Dutch Reformed Church.

What happened in France and Holland was happening in other countries. Roman Catholics and Protestants fought against each other in cruel wars that were far from Christian. This was because religion was all mixed up with governments and rulers. Many good people on both sides would not have chosen to settle questions of the Christian faith by killing one another but they seemed helpless. It was as though a great earthquake was rocking all Europe. The Church split in two. Protestant Churches were strongest in the north, while the Roman Catholic Church still controlled the southern countries.

The Church of England had been Protestant for many years, but some people thought it was not Protestant enough. These people, who had studied with Calvin and Knox, found fault with the forms and customs which the English Church followed. "The Church of England is no different from the Roman Church," they objected. "We must have a purely Protestant Church and not one which is more than half Roman Catholic." These people were called Puritans.

When James, the son of Mary Queen of Scots, became king of England, he disappointed many of the Puritans, who thought he would be a Presbyterian. The Catholics were sure he would be a Roman Catholic like his mother. But James wanted neither Presbyterian nor Roman rule. He chose the Church of England, of which he would be the head, and he paid

no attention to all the reforms that the Puritans asked him to make. He did, however, approve a new and better translation of the Bible, which became known as the King James Version. The finest scholars of the day were selected to do this work. It is used today all over the English-speaking world, and no other translation has more beautiful or stately language.

Some of the Puritans thought that Churches should be governed, not by bishops or presbyteries, but by congregations, who could choose their own leaders and work together in brotherly helpfulness. Many of them left England and went to Holland, some to that same town of Leyden which had defeated the Spanish army. Holland believed in letting people think and worship in peace.

"Weren't they the Pilgrims—who came to Plymouth on the Mayflower?" Joan asked.

"Yes, and pretty soon we shall be meeting them in New England," answered Mr. Wells.

Meanwhile the Puritans in England had a hard time reforming the Church, but they never stopped trying. They became more and more strict. They found fault with many popular amusements, particularly the sports which the king allowed after church on Sunday. "The Bible tells us to 'remember the sabbath day, to keep it holy,'" said the Puritans, "so it must be a day of worship and rest." They also objected to the special dress worn by the clergy, and they did

128

not like the Prayer Book. "Prayer should come from the heart and not from a book," they said.

The archbishop of Canterbury made a rule that all England must use the Prayer Book, and, since England and Scotland were united the king ordered the churches of Scotland to use it too.

"Oh, no!" said the Scots who were using a prayer book that John Knox had prepared for them. "We are Presbyterians, and shall go on worshiping in our own way." When a minister in Edinburgh tried to carry out the archbishop's order, he started a riot.

"One woman threw her stool at the minister's head," said Janet.

"She did?" Michael and Don grinned at each other.

"That wasn't very nice," said Ann. "He was only doing what he'd been told to do."

"People do foolish and unkind things when they lose their tempers," Mother said. "The Scots were very angry at being told to make changes in the way they worshiped."

All these quarrels led to war in which both Scots and English fought against the king. But after a few years, the Puritans who refused to follow the forms and rules of the Church of England were forced out of it. They were not free to worship together in their own way. Unless they used the service of the Prayer Book they were severely punished by imprisonment or worse. Hundreds of ministers had their churches taken away from them.

For nearly thirty years the dark and dirty prisons of England were full of good men whose only crime was loyalty to their own belief. Many prisoners were Quakers, whose leader was George Fox. The Quakers did not follow the forms used in any of the Churches. "God's voice speaks to our hearts," said George Fox, "and we do not need outside help to hear him. When we meet together we will sit and listen in silence until God's Spirit tells us what we are to say or do." The Quakers would not go to war and they refused to take the oaths which the law required. Hundreds of them met their death in prison.

A few years later, England had a king and queen who were wise enough to believe that different forms of worship could exist side by side in peace. They passed a law giving freedom of worship to all Protestants.

"It was time they did!" Joan spoke indignantly. "Churches ought to be friendly."

"It was the kings and queens who made all the trouble in those days," said Ann.

Don looked thoughtful. "People seemed to think more of their Church than anything else."

"That's why so many crossed the ocean to America in little leaky boats," said Michael.

11. The Church in a New World

Dry leaves whirled and eddied around the tree roots. A few bright fall flowers still nodded on their withered stalks. Joan and Ann, coming home from school, walked where the leaves lay thickest. They liked the crackling sound under their feet.

"It's fun to go away for a vacation, but it's even more fun to come home." Joan gave a little skip.

"Yes," Ann agreed, "everything seems new and exciting again after you've been away for six weeks."

"Oh, look," exclaimed Joan, "there's the new church! Didn't they do a lot while we were gone?"

"Yes," Ann looked as pleased as though it were her own church. Then she added: "I saw where the first church in Virginia was built. We went there this summer."

"You did? That's funny, because I went to Plymouth, where the Pilgrims built their first church. We'll tell Mr. Wells about it when he comes over tonight."

"What a fine reunion!" Mr. Wells looked around the living room where the firelight flickered on tanned faces and bright eyes. "Vacation time seems to have agreed with everyone. Perhaps you would like to hear about my vacation in California and some old mission churches I saw there."

Not long after Christopher Columbus came to our shores, many white-winged ships were sailing westward. Reports of the land that Columbus had discovered pleased King Ferdinand and Queen Isabella of Spain so much that they soon sent out other explorers to seek lands and treasure.

As Spain was a Roman Catholic country, the pope also took an interest in these expeditions. "Wherever Spanish ships sail," said the pope, "there too the Church shall go." So, while many people in northern Europe were turning to the Protestant faith, an army of monks and priests were sent to teach the Roman Catholic faith to the natives of the Western world.

Like great white birds, Spanish galleons swept across the seas, dipping in and out among the islands of blue Caribbean waters, or skimming on to the shores of North and South America. Others dropped anchor along the coasts of Panama, Mexico, and Florida. The Indians gazed in surprise as explorers and monks swarmed ashore to set up a cross and claim these lands for Spain and for the pope.

Some pushed west across miles and miles of wilderness until, after long years of hardship and struggle, the west coast was reached. "New Spain," they called this vast territory. After a time, in place of the adventurers who went back to Europe with gold and treasure, people from Spain and Portugal came to stay. They built cities and cathedrals like those of the Old World. Mexico City, the finest of these cities of New

Spain, was the capital of this new land.

One New Year's Day, Junípero Serra came limping into Mexico City. He had tramped three hundred miles over rough and dangerous country, climbing at last to the capital, eight thousand feet above the sea. But Mexico City reminded Father Serra too much of the gay Spanish cities of the Old World. He was not satisfied to preach in the cathedral, with its gold and silver statues. He wanted to go into the wilderness and teach Christianity to the Indians. No mountain trail was too hard for his feet, and no stream too dangerous for his canoe, even when wild beasts lurked in the thickets or mosquitoes rose in swarms before his eyes. On he went, planting crosses in the wilderness and telling the Indians the story of Christ. He learned their language and taught them to grow food and weave clothing for themselves.

After a few years Father Serra left Mexico to go with a company of pioneer settlers to California. It was a beautiful shore that the pioneers had come to settle. Green hills sloped down to curving beaches and sparkling blue bays. Sometimes the masts of a Spanish ship rocked gently with the tide or the canoes of Indian fishermen darted lightly to and fro. Everywhere were vines heavy with grapes, fields carpeted with yellow poppies, and roses without number.

For fifteen years Father Serra limped back and forth between the nine missions which he had founded. Although they were not always easy to win, Father

Serra's work and love for the Indians never faltered. *"Amar a Dios"* ("Love God") were the first Spanish words he taught them, and this became the greeting of Indian and Spaniard alike. The Indians learned to cut stone and to make tiles; they built lovely fountains, hung bells, and made altars and pews for the little churches. Toward the end of his life, Father Serra could count thousands of dark-skinned Christians whom his patience and love had brought into the Church, and today many people stop to visit the missions and hear the story of the faithful padres who cared more for God and their red brothers than for all the gold that explorers carried back to Spain.

While Spanish explorers were claiming most of the New World for Spain, the king of France was saying: "Why should Spain and Portugal divide the New World between them? France has just as much right to America as they have!"

There were plenty of Frenchmen ready for adventure and soon French ships were sailing westward. Within a few years all the Atlantic Coast, from Florida to the Saint Lawrence River, was called New France. Then up the Saint Lawrence into the heart of the continent went the ships, and with them went the Jesuits—another order of monks—to spread the teachings of the Roman Catholic Church among the Indians. They worked among tribes of Indians that were strong and warlike, much fiercer than those of California. The Jesuits were often tortured or killed, but still they moved in and out of Indian camps and villages, living as the Indians did, while teaching them the Christian faith.

Most of the trouble with the Indians was stirred up by soldiers and traders. Instead of treating the Indians kindly, as did the Jesuits and Franciscans, these men cheated them in trading and sold them firearms and liquor. After a while Indian wars swept away the missions that the Jesuits had worked so hard to establish. No sign of them was left.

"All of America was either New Spain or New France then!" exclaimed Michael. "What if it had stayed that way?"

"But it didn't!" cried Joan. "The Pilgrims were coming!"
"I think," said Mother, "God had his own plan for America."

The Pilgrims were not the first Protestants to come to America. More than fifty years earlier stories of sunny Florida had come to the ears of the persecuted Huguenots of France. *There*, they thought, *is the place we are looking for to build a peaceful home.* But the Huguenot settlements did not turn out very well. They not only had trouble with the Indians, but they found the Spaniards also ready to pounce on them and drive them out. "Are these Protestants from France planning to settle in the New World? We'll soon put an end to that!" exclaimed Philip II of Spain, when he heard that the Huguenots were landing in Florida. So he sent his most able general, who attacked them with terrible cruelty, and the little Huguenot colonies were destroyed.

On a spring day in the year 1607, Captain John Smith brought his ship to anchor and landed one hundred and five Englishmen on a marshy strip of Virginia. The blossoming shore seemed calm and peaceful after five months of tossing on the stormy Atlantic, but a lot of hard work had to be done before they could rest. Even before they had a roof over their heads, the colonists had a church. Robert Hunt, a minister of the Church of England, had come with them as a chaplain. Nailing a board between two trees which rose

straight and tall as the spires of his cathedral in England, Hunt placed his Bible and Prayer Book upon it. Above he spread an old sail, torn and stained from many a voyage. This was his reading desk and pulpit, and here he held services every day until a better church could be built.

"I saw where that first church was built," Ann could not help interrupting. "It was at Jamestown. There's an old tower still standing, but it belonged to a church that was built afterward—on the same spot."

"Yes," said Mr. Wells, "I've seen it too."

Life was hard and dangerous for a long time. Half of the colonists died the first winter. But King James sent other expeditions from England to Virginia, and gradually things grew better. A new church was built, with two bells on top which were rung every morning for early worship. Everyone, from the governor down, was expected to be there, and on Sunday and Thursday the governor appeared in his robes of state, with his council and fifty soldiers in red cloaks marching behind.

In faraway Leyden, where they had been living with the Dutch people, the Pilgrims began to hear stories about the English colony in Virginia. "We too," they decided, "will seek a new home in America. We will ask King James to give us a grant of land in Virginia, where our English countrymen are doing so well." But King James didn't want any people in Virginia who had separated from the Church of England, so the Pilgrims had to make other plans.

At last, on a September day in the year 1620, they set sail in the *Mayflower*. On and on they went, one hundred men, women, and children, with only stout

hearts and a dream of freedom to help them win their three months' battle with the sea. When Atlantic storms tore at the sails and angry waves broke over the decks of the *Mayflower*, there must have been many who thought longingly of the green fields of England. They huddled together in the cabin and prayed that God would bring them in safety to their new home.

No green and blossoming shore greeted the straining eyes of the weary Pilgrims when at last land was sighted. Winter was drawing near and the coast looked gray and bare. But they fell on their knees to thank God that soon they would once more have the firm earth under their feet. As they sailed into a quiet harbor, the leaders wrote out an agreement in which the Pilgrims promised to make laws for the good of all the colony, and to obey the leaders whom they should choose. This agreement was afterward called the Mayflower Compact. There was nothing in it about treasure to be gained or worldly honors to be won. The reason for their coming was plainly stated: ". . . for the glory of God, and advancement of the Christian faith."

It took six weeks for exploring parties to find the best location for the colony. Ice was in the bay and snow covered the ground when the right spot was finally chosen, and many more weeks were to pass before little homes were ready and the women and children could be landed from the *Mayflower*. But at last the brave Pilgrim band stood shivering on the shore. New Plymouth, the settlement was called, for that Plymouth far across the ocean which most of them would never see again.

When spring came, the *Mayflower* shook out her sails and made ready to depart for England. Now was the time for those who wanted to give up this struggle with disease and starvation to return to the Old World. Not a person went, although tears must have filled many eyes as they watched the *Mayflower* disappear in the gray sea mists. Now the last link with their former life was broken. But the sun was getting warmer day by day, and smoke was rising from the chimneys of little homes which the Pilgrim fathers had built for their families, so all took up the new life bravely.

The meetinghouse was now finished. It was a square building with a high, steep roof, thatched with sea grass. The Pilgrims had no minister. Church services in Plymouth were led by Elder Brewster. On Sunday and Thursday the roll of a drum called the Pilgrim fathers and their families to meet in front of Captain Standish's house. All wore their best clothes, and each man carried a musket. Three abreast they marched to church. Behind walked Governor Bradford, with Elder Brewster on his right hand and Captain Standish on his left. As they read the Bible and prayed and sang together, sharp black eyes were watching from the edge of the forest.

One day, to the Pilgrims' great surprise, an Indian came into the settlement. "Welcome, Englishmen," he said. This was Samoset, who had learned from codfishers to speak a few words of English. Samoset and another Indian, Squanto, tried to bring about friendliness between the Pilgrims and the Indians. A treaty of peace was signed which was not broken for fifty years. When the Pilgrims celebrated their first harvest with a feast of thanksgiving, they invited the Indians to join in the festival.

Meanwhile other ships came sailing into Plymouth harbor, bringing friends from England and Holland who had been left behind when the *Mayflower* sailed. And not many years later, when the Puritans gave up hope of ever being able to change the Church of England, many crossed the Atlantic Ocean to build their own churches on the shores of Massachusetts Bay at Boston and Salem. And that was the way in which Protestants made their homes all along the eastern coast of America.

"They couldn't call it New France any more," said Michael. "It was New England now."

"And New Amsterdam," Don reminded him. "My ancestors, the Dutch, settled there."

"And Virginia!" cried the three girls.

"When Luther nailed his paper to the door of the church at Wittenberg," said Father, "he didn't know that Columbus had already found a land where his teachings would take root and grow."

12. Sweet Land of Liberty

All the girls and boys came trooping into the living room. Mr. Wells wrinkled his nose and sniffed. "I like that autumn smell of smoke," he said. "What have you been up to?"

"We had a bonfire," Michael told him. "Don's father burned up all the dry leaves in their garden."

"What are you going to tell us about tonight, Mr. Wells?" Joan wanted to know.

"Something that I think will interest Janet," answered Mr. Wells. "Did you know, Janet, that some of the Scots were Irish too?"

Janet looked doubtful and shook her head. "A Scot's always a Scot," she declared firmly.

"Let's see how it happened that some of them were called Scotch-Irish," said Mr. Wells.

WHILE the English colonists at Jamestown were learning to shoulder an ax or a spade, the Scots had their eyes turned toward another shore. Only thirteen miles across the water lay the northern coast of Ireland, where English soldiers had driven out the Irish lords who had ruled there. The Irish people who were faithful to the Roman Catholic Church had been forced to move into the southern provinces, and King James was encouraging English and Scottish Protestants to settle in the north.

Many Scots were tired of having the churches and

government always at war with each other and they liked this idea. *Over in Ireland,* they thought, *we can build our homes and churches without fear. Our children will know the Christian liberty which John Knox taught us to fight for here in Scotland.* Thousands crossed the narrow passage to Ireland with high hopes of founding a free state, in which the Presbyterian Kirk of Scotland should not be under the rule of bishops or kings.

For many years all went well. The sturdy Scots knew how to farm and to build comfortable homes for their families. But there was trouble ahead for the Presbyterians in Ulster, as their settlement was called. Even there they could not escape the warfare and bloodshed into which the English kings plunged all Britain. At last many of the Scots, like the Puritans, sailed across the sea.

The Scots were not coming to a lonely, unknown shore such as the Pilgrims and Jamestown settlers had faced. The Puritan settlements on Massachusetts Bay had grown to be strong and thriving communities.

Farther south, settlements of English, Scottish, Dutch, and French Protestants dotted the green countrysides and the coast as far as Virginia.

Across the Potomac River a large tract of land had been given by the king to an Englishman who belonged to the Church of Rome, but who believed that

every follower of Christ should be free to worship in his own way.

"That was Lord Baltimore, who founded our own state of Maryland!" cried Joan.

"Yes," said Mr. Wells, "and it was through Lord Baltimore that so many of the Scots from Ireland came to Maryland."

"Did they really come here to Maryland?" Janet's eyes were bright with excitement.

Lord Baltimore wanted his colony to grow and prosper, so he promised land and freedom of religion to the settlers. Far off in Ulster the Scotch-Irish people heard about this, and soon ship after ship was on its way bringing the persecuted Scots to another new home. Among those who sailed into Chesapeake Bay was a Presbyterian minister from Ulster, named Francis Makemie. He was full of fire and energy, and started at once to build little Presbyterian churches all over Maryland.

"One of Makemie's churches may have stood where our own church is being built today," interrupted Father.

"Not the one that burned down?" Michael was figuring out the dates.

"No, that church was built after the Revolutionary War, but we have records showing that an older church was there first."

"Oh, I hope it was one of Makemie's churches!" Joan exclaimed.

Makemie didn't stay long in any one place. Like the apostles Peter and Paul, he went from town to town and settlement to settlement, preaching and founding churches, all the way from South Carolina to New York. New York now had an English governor who wanted all the people of New York to belong to the Church of England. One day Makemie was arrested and put in jail.

"You are preaching without the permission of the governor," he was told. "The Presbyterians have no license to preach in New York."

"Did the apostles ask if they might preach the Gospel of Jesus Christ?" Makemie asked in reply. After a trial Makemie was allowed to go free, although he had to pay a large fine.

By this time William Penn, a Quaker, had started
a colony. From the first there was a feeling of brother-
hood between the Quakers and the Indians. Under an
elm tree, with yellow autumn leaves falling on his
broad-brimmed hat and on the heads of the red men
grouped around him, Penn made a treaty which was
never broken. Pennsylvania became a home not only
for the Quakers but for persecuted people from Holland and Germany. Everyone was welcome, and free
to be a member of whatever Church he chose.

147

Meanwhile the Puritans were building Congregational churches on the village greens of towns all over New England. They were plain little churches, as different as possible from the stately churches of England and other countries of Europe. Made of wood and square in shape, they had a high shingled roof, with a belfry on top from which the call to worship rang out in commanding tones.

Inside the Puritan churches there were benches to sit on, and a table at one end with a chair behind it for the minister. Later they built pews instead of benches, and had a regular pulpit. Sometimes the pews were square, like boxes, and people were almost hidden. It was easy for members of the congregation to fall asleep when the sermon was too long, or the day was warm enough to make them drowsy. Children often took this opportunity to giggle or play tricks on each other. But not for long! A man whose duty it was to go around looking for such offenders would soon tap them on the head with his bone-headed rod.

The Puritans had been very strict in England, and they were even more strict in America. They had given up their homes and risked their lives to come to this new land. Now they wanted to be very sure that no beliefs but their own should be followed. "No one," said the Puritans, "who is not a member of our Church shall belong to our colony."

The people of Boston even drove one young minister, Roger Williams, out of Massachusetts. They did not agree with some of his opinions. "You must not take any of the Indians' land without their consent or without paying for it," said Williams. The Puritans thought the king's grant gave them the right to this land. Williams also said they should not compel people to go to church. Everybody in the colony knew that there would be serious trouble for anyone who stayed at home when the church bell rang. Williams even declared that the laws governing daily life should be separate from Church laws. That seemed foolish because the Church fathers were also the governors.

Driven away from Boston, Salem, and Plymouth, Roger Williams went into the forest to live with the Indians. It was winter, but the Indians were good to him and Williams bought from them a strip of land on Narragansett Bay. Here, when spring was smiling on the dunes and turning the water to sapphire blue, he started a settlement and called it "Providence," in thankfulness to God for his goodness.

And now Protestants of every kind gathered at Providence. It was called the Rhode Island Colony, and whoever came was sure of liberty to worship according to his own heart and conscience. Indians came and

went freely, for they knew that Roger Williams was their friend. It was his friendliness with the Indians that brought a messenger from the Puritans hurrying to Providence one day. "The Pequot tribe is about to attack our colony," gasped the messenger. "Won't you do what you can to help us?" Williams went at once into the camps of the hostile Indians and pleaded with them to make a friendly agreement with the Puritans. Because they trusted and liked him, they did what Williams asked.

For a while the Puritans didn't get along with the Pilgrims, but sickness drew them together. Disease struck at the Puritans when they had no doctor and very little medicine. Up the shore went Dr. Samuel Fuller, of Plymouth, with his remedies. He saved many lives, and healed not only their sickness but also the differences between the colonies. Governor Endecott, of Salem, wrote to Governor Bradford, of Plymouth: "I acknowledge myself bound to you for your kind love and care in sending Dr. Fuller among us . . . ." After that the New England colonies forgot the things that had divided them.

"Didn't anyone try to make Christians of the Indians?" Don asked.

"Oh, yes, many did! There was John Eliot, of Massachusetts, for instance."

John Eliot was called the "Apostle of the Indians."

He learned the language of the Algonquin Indians and made a translation of the Bible. "The Indians must be able to read the Bible in their own tongue," he said. This was the first Bible to be printed in America. Eliot worked out a plan for building little Indian villages near the colonies. "The Indians can learn the message of Christ better by seeing how Christian people live than by words," he reasoned. Soon there was a whole colony of Christian Indians, who were known as the "praying Indians." Eliot trained the Indians to be missionaries to their own people. When a cruel Indian war broke out later, the "praying Indians" stood between the hostile tribes and the colonists.

Schools went hand in hand with the Church in Massachusetts. The Puritans had been trained according to the ideas of that great schoolmaster of Geneva, John Calvin, who believed that education should begin with the very young. When Captain John Endecott brought sixty Puritans to Salem, among their number was a man who was to be the first schoolteacher in the colony. Francis Higginson had eight

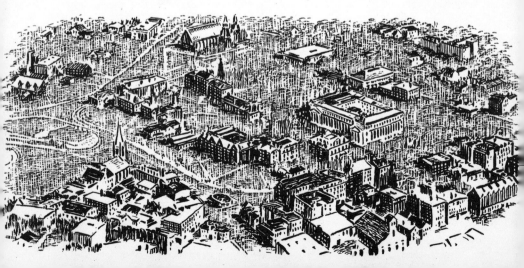

children of his own, and he knew how important it was to have a school. In less than ten years Higginson's school became Harvard College, the first Protestant college in America. Later other colleges were started to train young men to be ministers.

About this time an Irish Presbyterian minister, William Tennent, came to Pennsylvania. He had four sons, and had made up his mind that all should serve the Church. "The only good preachers are educated preachers," said William Tennent. "We must have *good* preachers in America." So Tennent started a school, which was called the "Log College." It grew and grew until, as the years went by, fifty colleges and universities sprang from this small beginning.

"Suppose—" Mr. Wells interrupted his own story—"suppose we were able to jump into a plane, turn back the sun two hundred years, and cruise low from north to south over the American colonies. What do you think we should see?"

"Huh! That's a funny idea," Michael chuckled. "They didn't even have steamboats or trains in those days. Imagine flying in a plane!"

"Imagine turning the sun back!" added Don. "But let's go!"

The British flag is flying from Maine to Florida, but under that flag live strong, independent people who know what it means to conquer the wilderness for the sake of a free Church, free schools for their children, and the right to plan for their own future.

Over the green hills, west or north or south—whichever way you look—you can see the slender spires of churches. Many are better built than the first little square meetinghouses. The churches of Puritan New England have weathercocks on their steeples instead of crosses, but here and there we see crosses too, showing that Episcopal or Roman Catholic congregations also worship in New England.

South along the coast a rider gallops, carrying mail from one busy seaport town to another. Smoke rises from the chimneys of mills and factories; farmers work in their fields; carpenters build barns to store the harvest; a blacksmith hammers sparks from his anvil and fits the shoe to the hoof of a patient plow horse. In the south, dark-skinned men and women are picking basket after basket of cotton and tobacco.

If it is Sunday the busy wharfs on the water front are empty, and sails hang limply against the masts of the vessels. Streets and roads and fields are deserted, for neither farmer nor mill hand, carpenter nor blacksmith, work on the "Sabbath Day." The sound of church bells echoes from one end of the land to the other, as people come quietly out of their homes and turn toward the church. Children with well-washed faces, mothers and fathers wearing their best clothing, all answer the call of the church bells: Congregationalists, Baptists, Presbyterians, Episcopalians, Lutherans, Quakers, Huguenots, Roman Catholics.

"It didn't really matter that the churches had so many names," said Don, "when they all felt the same way about important things."

"I didn't know the Church did so much to make our country great"— Michael spoke as though he had just discovered something. "I guess we were Christians first and Americans afterward."

13. Preachers on Horseback

Father unrolled a drawing and spread it out on the living room table. "Would you like to see a picture of our new church as it will look when it is finished?" he asked.

"Yes—yes—yes," the children's voices answered him as they crowded around the table.

Janet examined the drawing with interest. "We have churches like that in Scotland," she said.

"It looks something like my church too," Ann added.

"Yes, this is a style of church you would find in the villages of England and Scotland," Father told them. "It will make us think of our beginnings in the Old World. And here—" Father put his finger on a building adjoining the church— "is our church of tomorrow."

Michael turned a puzzled face to Father. "What do you mean—our church of tomorrow?"

"This will be our church school," answered Father, "and the place for all the doings of girls and boys and young people. You are the church of the future, aren't you?"

"Oh, that's right!" Michael's eyes followed the drawing as Father put it where all could see it while Mr. Wells talked.

MORE than two hundred years had passed since Martin Luther startled Europe wide awake by saying that the Church was wrong and ought to be reformed. Now people in Luther's Germany and in other parts of the world were again saying much the same thing. "The churches," they declared, "are wrong to spend their time arguing about creeds when they should be teaching the Bible. Our preachers tell us what to believe and the reasons why such beliefs are true, but they say very little about how to live with kindness and love for one another." These people didn't mean that creeds were not necessary, but they thought that living according to a creed was more important than talking about it.

Christian people began to hold meetings for Bible-reading and prayer. They hoped that their hearts would become so full of the Spirit of Jesus Christ that the heart of the Church, which seemed to have grown cold, might be kindled and made warm through them. Lives of such goodness and devotion to the Bible soon did make a difference in what preachers and teachers were saying. Many ministers began to look into their own hearts and to preach a simple faith that would help people to think and live as Christians.

About this time several students at Oxford University in England formed a club. They too felt that the Church had lost its warmth and spirit. "The best way to help the Church," they decided, "is to make our own lives better. Let us plan a program of study, prayer, and service to others, and keep strictly to it." The rest of the students at the university laughed at them and called their club the "Holy Club." Afterward someone thought up the name "Methodist," because such a strict method was followed by these young men in their daily life. John and Charles Wesley had

been leaders in this "Holy Club" until a plea for preachers came from the new colony of Georgia in America. With two other members of the club, the Wesleys then set sail for the New World.

On the voyage, a fierce storm struck terror into the hearts of all except some missionaries who were on the ship. *They have more courage and trust in God than I have,* thought John Wesley. *They must be better Christians.* Two years later, when he went back to England because he felt he had failed in Georgia, another missionary helped him find new courage.

Although John Wesley was a minister of the Church of England, he was not at all sure that he had enough fire in his own heart to win others to Christ. *How can I find the trust and joy which I need?* he wondered. Then one evening Wesley went to a prayer meeting and suddenly felt that God's Spirit had entered his heart, driving away all his doubts and fears. He rushed out to share this wonderful new feeling with his friends. "It's like being born again!" he cried.

Wesley's brother, Charles, and George Whitefield, another member of the Holy Club, had also felt this new fire in their hearts. All three started out to put new life into the Church. But the Church didn't want to hear such preaching and closed its doors to them.

"We can preach outdoors," said John Wesley. "We will go to the poor and see if they will listen when we tell them of a peace and happiness they have never known before."

There were plenty of poor in England. Three quarters of the people were living in poverty, while the rest were rich and many of them without kindness or pity. Whole families were sometimes thrown into jail because they could not pay their debts. Women and children, as well as men, worked in coal mines and factories. They had forgotten there was such a thing as the love of God until the Wesleys and George Whitefield came to tell them how Jesus Christ was God's gift of love to man. People listened with a new hope lighting up their tired eyes.

Sometimes mobs broke up their meetings because they preached against drunkenness and slavery. Many a time Wesley barely escaped death at the hands of such mobs, but on he went, bravely spreading his good news through England, Scotland, Wales, and Ireland. He bought a horse and rode over the rough roads, worn into ruts by the stagecoach, or along trails that were no more than goat tracks. He had to have help, so he trained carefully chosen men and called them "lay preachers." Soon a small army of horseback riders were traveling throughout the length and breadth of the British Isles, preaching, teaching, and singing. Towns that had been the roughest became respectable. There were schools for the children, homes for orphans and widows, places where medicine for the sick was given to all who needed it.

Then the Methodists came to America, which like Germany and England, had been growing careless and cold in its religious life. The first settlers were gone, and their children and grandchildren had not the same stern faith that had conquered the wilderness. Life was now easier and the Church didn't mean so much to them. Most of the ministers preached what they thought people wanted to hear instead of the strict Puritan beliefs.

Jonathan Edwards, the minister of a church in Northampton, Massachusetts, looked down from his pulpit into the faces of the congregation. *They won't like it,* he thought, *if I tell them about their sins, or how cold their hearts are, or that they are only half awake. Probably they will refuse to pay my salary if I make them angry, but that shall not stop me.* So Jonathan Edwards went on to preach his famous sermon "Sinners in the Hands of an Angry God."

People sat up straighter and listened. They were wide awake now. They began to think of themselves as sinners, and to wonder how God would punish them. Parson Edwards was saying things that frightened them. Before he finished, women were weeping and men groaned aloud in distress. "What must we do to be saved?" they cried. Jonathan Edwards gave them the same answer that Peter gave at Pentecost: "If you repent and believe in Jesus Christ, God will forgive your sins and send his Holy Spirit into your hearts."

People now began to go to church not only on Sunday but every day in the week. A new feeling about religion swept from town to town like a flame. It spread over New England and reached other colonies. Meetings were held everywhere—"revival meetings," they were called, because they made thousands of men and women want to live a new life. This revival in the Church came to be known as the Great Awakening.

The Methodists had no pulpits to preach from at first, but they had the open air and the forest, where pine trees rose like church spires, and the green trails were like the quiet aisles of a great cathedral. They preached in "camp meetings," where their pulpit was a rude platform in a clearing, and the congregation sat on planks laid across tree stumps. Men who worked in mines and men of the wilderness saw them coming, and put down their pickaxes and saws to gather for a service. Sometimes the Methodist riders followed covered wagon trains all the way across the continent to the Pacific Coast.

John Wesley had started the first Sunday school in America at Savannah, Georgia. He knew how important it was for children to learn what was in the Bible while they were young. If they did not know what was in it, how could they be taught to follow the Bible's teaching? Wesley also thought that children should learn to pray and sing as he and his brothers and sisters had been taught by their parents.

They must have sung the hymns that were written by Isaac Watts, a Congregational minister in England. Some of these had very plain and pointed lessons. Children who were quarrelsome, for instance, might be taught to sing:

> "Let dogs delight to bark and bite,
>   For God hath made them so;
>   Let bears and lions growl and fight,
>   For 'tis their nature to.

> "But children, you should never let
>   Such angry passions rise;
>   Your little hands were never made
>   To tear each other's eyes."

"What a funny hymn!" Ann giggled.
"I guess they got the point all right," Michael grinned.

164

Sunday schools got their start in England. The children of miners and factory workers were getting no education at all, because they had to work all day, and every day, except Sunday. "Well then," said Robert Raikes, "we will have schools for them on Sunday, when they are free. We will hire teachers not only to teach these children to read, write, and do arithmetic, but also to tell them about Jesus." Dirty, overworked children began to have clean faces and a new light in their eyes, and soon Sunday schools were a part of Church life all over England.

In America too Sunday schools became popular. After a while only Christian teaching and training were given in the Sunday schools because there were day schools to take care of other kinds of study. But the Sunday schools had come to stay and to grow. Millions of children all over the world have been enrolled as members.

Joan looked up at the picture over the mantel. "I hope we'll make our Sunday school the best in the whole world!" she declared.

"You don't have to wait for the new church," Father's eyes twinkled as he spoke. "You can start next Sunday!"

14. Into All the World

"Here's a picture Uncle Tom made for us last night." Joan held up the drawing for Mr. Wells to see. "It's a church on an island in the Pacific. He landed there with his parachute when his bomber was shot down."

Mr. Wells looked at the picture with interest. "A good many flyers owe their lives to the fact that men and women went to the South Sea Islands with the Gospel. What a nice church it is! It must have been built by the islanders. See, it has a roof of thatch, and the walls are probably of woven bamboo."

"What made missionaries start going way out there in the first place?" asked Don.

"They remembered what Jesus told his disciples to do," answered Mr. Wells, "and they wanted to obey him. 'Go ye into all the world,' said Jesus, 'and preach the gospel to every creature.'"

Soon after George Washington became the first President of the United States a little ship rode at anchor off the coast of England. The setting sun gilded her patched sails and brightened the faded letters on her hull. *"T-h-e D-u-f-f,"* spelled out the sailors on other vessels, wondering where this small ship could be going and what kind of cargo she carried.

It would have surprised them if they had been told that her cargo was missionaries. They probably had never heard of a missionary, and might have thought the word meant anything from a strange kind of fish to an African slave. They couldn't be expected to understand why men and women should want to take the good news of Jesus Christ halfway around the world!

Many Church people didn't understand any better. While nearly two thirds of the world had never heard of Christ, some Church leaders were saying, "We can't do anything about that; we have enough to do at home."

There were others who did not agree. "If we are to obey the command of Jesus to 'go into all the world,'" they said, "something *must* be done, and we are ready to do it." They formed small groups called missionary societies to send men and women to these faraway places with the Gospel. In the cabin of *The Duff* were eighteen missionaries whom the London Missionary Society was sending to Tahiti, an island in the South Seas.

The first American settlers had a short voyage compared with the one that was ahead of *The Duff* when she sailed out of the harbor. South and west, on and on, she sailed while the weeks and months flew by like the foaming water under her keel. Cape Horn was reached, and beyond stretched the Pacific Ocean. But here the wind blew such a gale that the ship was in danger. "We shall have to turn back!" shouted the captain as he and his crew struggled with the sails. So back they went—way back across the Atlantic Ocean from the tip of South America to the southern tip of Africa. Rounding the Cape of Good Hope, they sailed east for thousands of miles without seeing land or sighting more than a single sail.

At last one evening they saw mountains outlined against the sky. "Is that the island we're going to? Is that Tahiti?" cried the children who were in the party. They were beginning to feel that there was no land anywhere. "Yes," answered the captain, "you will be there when you wake up tomorrow morning."

Sure enough, before their eyes were half open, *The Duff* was gliding into a quiet bay. Out from the shore shot canoes filled with dark-skinned natives. "What will they do?" the missionaries asked each other, thinking anxiously of their wives and children. But the brown faces were friendly as they swarmed up the sides of the ship and stared at the white people. "We look as strange to them as they do to us," said the captain trying to give courage to the children, who were gazing wide-eyed from behind their mothers' skirts.

It was not long before the king and queen of Tahiti gave the missionaries land on which to build houses for themselves. There under the palm trees, on a shore thousands and thousands of miles from their English homeland, they began to teach the Gospel of Jesus Christ. In time others went to the South Seas—German, British, and American missionaries, both Protestant and Catholic. From island to island they went, carrying their Bibles and the message of one great Father who loved all men. The native people began to turn from idols to worship this Father and his Son, Jesus Christ.

Today on hundreds of little islands that dot Pacific waters, bells ring out the hour of worship in Christian churches and thousands of dark heads are bent in prayer. The praises of Jesus, whose good news came to their island through missionary preachers, teachers, and doctors, are sung in many languages.

"What if they had never gone!" Joan was thinking of Uncle Tom and other flyers who might have dropped from the sky into the midst of a cannibal feast, instead of finding Christian natives who were ready to help them.

"The Church might not have gone farther than Jerusalem, or Antioch, or Damascus," said Mr. Wells, "but then it wouldn't

170

have been the kind of Church Jesus meant it to be. His Church was to go into all the world. The Church has sometimes forgotten that, but there have always been men and women who did not forget. Shall I tell you about a few more of them?"

"Yes!" The vote was unanimous.

A little while before *The Duff* set sail, a young cobbler sat at his bench making shoes. "Rat-a-tat" went his hammer and in and out flashed his sharp needle, but William Carey's thoughts were very far away from the English town where he lived. His eyes often went to a map which hung on the wall. He had made the map himself, and took many imaginary journeys while his fingers were busy with his work and his feet moved never an inch away from his bench.

"Have you been round the world with Captain Cook today?" a friend asked, stopping in the doorway of his shop.

Carey smiled and shook his head. "No," he said, "I've just been as far as India today."

India was a land of great riches, as traders had long ago discovered, and it was the home of millions of people who had never heard the name of Christ. As his friend passed on, Carey turned the page of a Latin grammar, which was lying with the Bible on the bench beside him. *I must study all the languages I can*, he thought. *I want to give the people of India and other Eastern lands a Bible in their own language someday*. Soon afterward Carey became a minister, although he still supported his family by making shoes.

Meanwhile a small group of Baptist ministers met together to talk over a daring plan. "William Carey is right," they said. "If we 'attempt great things for God' we can 'expect great things from God.' Let us form a society to spread the Gospel all around the world." They had only about sixty-three dollars altogether—but they went ahead making plans. A few months later William Carey and his family were sent to India.

They found India to be a land of cruel and barbarous customs. One was that of marrying little girls to older husbands. When the husband died, the child widow was burned alive on the same fire with her dead husband. "This is murder!" protested Carey. "It must be stopped!" "We have been doing this for hundreds of years," he was told. "You can never change our customs." It took a long time, but before Carey died the governor decreed that the burning of child widows should cease.

During the forty-one years that Carey was in India, he wrote letter after letter to people in England telling of his work. At last the Church was awakened. Missionary societies were formed to send the Gospel to every land, and many young men and women offered to go as missionaries. One of them, Robert Morrison, sailed for China.

A few years earlier, visitors to the British Museum in London might have noticed a young man poring

over two old manuscripts and writing on a piece of
paper. If they had been bold enough to ask him what
he was doing, Robert Morrison would have explained
that these were Chinese manuscripts and that he was
teaching himself the Chinese language. Probably the
visitors would have wondered why anyone should
want to learn Chinese, but Morrison kept right on
copying page after page every day. Each strange-
looking character he copied was a word, and there
were 40,000 words to learn. When at last he was able
to read and write this difficult language, Morrison
studied to be a minister. The London Missionary
Society sent him as their first missionary to China.

China was a country with a very old civilization.
One out of every four people in the world lived there,
and they had religions of their own dating back four
thousand years. The Chinese didn't want to hear
about the "Jesus religion." Morrison was forbidden to
preach at all. "Well, then," said Morrison, "I will get
right to work on a translation of the Bible, and when
the Chinese people are willing to listen, there will be
a Chinese Bible ready for them." After a time the
Chinese Government was not so strict, and Morrison
was able to preach the Gospel. But, like Carey, at the
end of his life he could count only a small number
whom he had won to Christ.

Meanwhile another young man, Robert Moffat,
had gone to South Africa as a missionary when he
was twenty-one. "Look out for Afrikaner," Moffat was

warned when he first reached Africa; "he will make a drum of your skin and use your skull for a drinking cup." But Moffat went straight to this African chief's village and made a friend of him, and later a Christian. Meanwhile, Moffat was trying to learn an African language. He couldn't study it out of a book. So bit by bit he made up an alphabet and built words that would sound like the native speech. Then he wrote a spelling book and a catechism, and translated the Bible into the words which he had created.

When, after twenty years, Moffat went to England to have his New Testament printed, a young Scottish doctor, David Livingstone, heard him tell the story of his work in Africa. "I have sometimes seen in the morning sun the smoke of a thousand villages where no missionary has ever been," said Moffat. David Livingstone's heart was stirred. He had been planning to go to China, but now he made up his mind to go to this Dark Continent, with its unexplored jungles and masses of black people who needed Christ.

Up and down rivers and through jungles, where no other white man had been, went Livingstone. On and on he traveled—exploring and making maps, while at the same time he was healing disease and telling the story of Jesus. His skill as a doctor made the savage tribes friendly.

One day Livingstone walked into the great slave market at Zanzibar, on the east coast of Africa, and saw hundreds of men and women being bargained for and sold. His reports aroused the people of Britain to action, and Queen Victoria made the sultan of Zanzibar give orders that the slave market should stop. Today in that same market place a great church stands. It was built by Negro hands, and within its walls Negro ministers preach the Gospel of Christ.

Livingstone died in the heart of Africa. Even Henry Stanley, who went to Africa to find him, couldn't get him to go home while his work was unfinished. Other explorers and missionaries followed the trails broken by Livingstone—trails 29,000 miles long—through forest and swamp. And often along the way, or beside a campfire, they heard natives tell of the great man "who was different from any other man because he loved everyone."

"How about America?" asked Michael. "Didn't the Churches here send any missionaries to Africa or Asia or the South Seas?"

"We're just coming to that," answered Mr. Wells.

175

"American Churches have done a great deal to send the Gospel around the world. It all began with a group of college boys caught in a shower."

They were talking about William Carey in India, these students of Williams College, and about Robert Morrison, who had lately gone to China. Long purple shadows darkened the mountains and crept into the grove where they lay stretched out under the trees, thinking of these faraway lands.

"There's Africa too," said Samuel Mills, "and the islands out in the South Pacific. Just think of the millions who have never heard of Christ! They need missionaries so badly in all these places. "Why"— Samuel Mills sat up—"why shouldn't we go?"

"Who would send us?" one of the other boys asked. "The Church has no foreign missions."

"We must pray about it," said a third student. "God will surely show us the way if he wants us to do this work."

The rumble of thunder rolled along the mountains and a gust of wind drove raindrops into their faces. The young men jumped to their feet. "The haystack!" cried Mills, and they raced for its shelter just as the rain came down in torrents. While they waited for the shower to be over, they pledged themselves to take the Gospel to foreign lands, and prayed that God would open the way. Later they prepared themselves for this work by studying to be ministers.

Meanwhile, they wrote a letter to a group of ministers meeting for a conference. They told of their plan and asked the help and prayers of the churches. Very soon the first foreign missionary society was organized, and two years later five young missionaries, with their brides, were on their way to the Far East.

Samuel Mills didn't go with his friends. He saw that there was work that must be done at home first. Missionaries must take Bibles with them to foreign lands, so he formed a Bible Society to translate and print Bibles in all the known languages. He also planned other societies for world-wide missions.

About this time people from Europe were crowding into American cities, particularly the big ports like New York, and there were not enough homes for them. Often several families lived in one or two rooms, causing all kinds of sickness. Mills helped start city missions to take care of these foreign-born people, and he did a great deal to help the Negroes.

At last Samuel Mills started for Africa. He was ready and eager to begin the great adventure for Christ which he had planned for so long. But he stayed only long enough to choose a place for a mission colony, which he never saw, for he died on the return voyage.

"Oh, dear!" Joan's voice was distressed, and everyone else looked sad at this unexpected turn in the story.

"Even if he didn't do all that he had planned, the work he began grew and grew," said Mr. Wells, "like a great snow-ball rolling across America and around the world. During the next hundred years the Church took the Gospel of Jesus Christ to nearly every land on earth."

"Wouldn't that bring us almost up to our own day?" asked Father.

Mr. Wells nodded. "We'll soon be getting into the story ourselves."

15. One Great Fellowship

Midge scampered out into the hall and barked at the front door.

"I guess Mr. Wells is coming." Michael left the rest of the group and ran to open the door.

"That fire looks fine! There's frost in the air tonight," said Mr. Wells, coming into the living room with Michael. "I'm sorry to be late, but we had a meeting to hear reports on the new church."

"How is it going?" Father asked.

"Better than we expected," answered Mr. Wells, "and that is something we want to thank God for on Thanksgiving Day."

"Last week," Michael reminded him, "you said we'd soon be in the story of the Church ourselves."

"So we shall." Mr. Wells settled himself in the chair that Father had pushed closer to the fire. "But we don't want to skip those hundred years when the Church was pushing its great missionary snowball around the world. Something an Indian brave said started it rolling across our own country."

MY PEOPLE sent me to get the white man's Book of Heaven, but you have given me other things instead. I am going back to them without the Book, and my people will die in darkness." The Indian brave was speaking to the commander of a military post at St. Louis. With three other Indians he had journeyed "many moons from the setting sun," over trails thou-

sands of miles long, in search of a Book which he hoped would bring light to his people, but he had failed to find it.

In a little village of western New York, young Dr. Whitman read about these Indians. The words of the Indian brave stirred him deeply. "What a cry for help!" Whitman exclaimed. "The Bible—the 'white man's Book of Heaven'—must be taken to them!"

On the Fourth of July, when the Declaration of Independence was just sixty years old, a long caravan wound through a pass at the summit of the Rocky Mountains and came out on the Pacific slope. At the end of the caravan a battered wagon, drawn by two mules, bumped and lurched over the rough ground as though it might turn upside down any moment. But Marcus Whitman had done what everyone said was impossible: he had driven the first wagon over the Rockies. Whitman's wife and another young woman, the bride of one of the two missionaries with him, forgot all the hardship they had suffered, in the thrill of knowing that they were the first white women to cross these great peaks. They gazed with shining eyes at the broad lands stretched out before them.

Two more months of braving the wilderness, climbing mountains, and fording rivers, but at last their long journey came to an end. On the bank of a little river in Oregon, Marcus Whitman built his home and began to work among the Indians. "You have brought the Book of Heaven?" they asked him. And Whitman showed them the Bible, which he had carried three thousand miles that they might have the Gospel of Christ.

Soon fields of wheat, corn, and potatoes were planted, and a mill was built to grind the grain. The Indians saw that these missionaries could not only preach and pray; they could also work with their hands. While her husband was building, planting, and taking care of the sick, Mrs. Whitman started a school for the Indian children.

181

Whitman went east again and piloted a thousand men, women, and children, with hundreds of wagons, oxen, and cattle, back over the Rockies to Oregon. He believed that Americans should settle there and make it part of the United States. Finally a treaty was signed giving Oregon to the United States. Meanwhile Dr. and Mrs. Whitman went on with their work among the Indians until they lost their lives in a massacre. On that dreadful day sixteen white people were killed or taken captive by Indians whom the Whitmans had tried so hard to help.

"Why?" cried Ann.

"A number of things had stirred up the Indians. One was an epidemic of measles in which many died. The Indians thought Dr. Whitman had poisoned them so that the white people might have their land."

"How could they think anything so foolish, when he had done so much for them!"

"Many white people had been guilty of robbing the Indians of their land, so they were suspicious even of the missionaries. We cannot blame them too much if they often did not know who were their friends and who were not."

Twenty years after the Whitmans were killed, the United States Government bought from Russia a large piece of land in the northwest—much farther away than Oregon. Many people thought it was spending money foolishly to buy a land of snow and ice. "That polar bear garden," some called it. They

had no idea that Alaska would bring great riches in minerals, furs, and fish to their country.

Before very long the Church sent missionaries to Alaska. They were no more afraid of ice and snow than Livingstone had been of the hot jungles of Africa. With dog team and sled they "mushed" over mountains and through forests. They didn't dare to ride, for they would have frozen to death with the thermometer sixty degrees below zero.

A Presbyterian missionary explorer, Sheldon Jackson, had been the first to go. He was building churches in the west when he saw a letter written by an American soldier stationed in Alaska. "We need missionaries to help these Eskimo and Indian people," said the letter. Sheldon Jackson started at once.

"Schools are what they need most," said Jackson, when he saw how ignorant and helpless these people were, and how they were cheated and abused by white men who came to get all the riches they could from this vast new country. So from village to village he went, crossing glaciers and plunging through trackless wastes of snow, building one school after another.

Jackson soon discovered that the natives were dying of starvation. Fishing fleets and traders had driven off or destroyed the fish and wild animals on which

the natives depended for food. What could be done to help them? Across the narrow Bering Sea lay Siberia, where herds of reindeer roamed. *Why not bring some of these animals over to Alaska*, thought Jackson, *and let the Eskimos and Indians raise them for food?* Presbyterian churches sent him money and Jackson went to Siberia. He brought back a herd of reindeer, and saved the Alaskans from a slow death.

Men and women from many churches followed Jackson to Alaska. They went into rough mining camps; they built churches, schools, and hospitals in desolate places. There were never enough missionaries or money to do all that was needed.

Far to the south, the Church saw other work to do. There were four million Negroes freed from slavery who didn't know how to use their new freedom. Schools had to be started where they could be taught. One of the largest schools was at Hampton, Virginia. One day a thirteen-year-old boy came to Hampton in search of an education. He was given a job as janitor so that he could pay for his studies. When he graduated, they made him a teacher, and finally he started a school of his own. Booker T. Washington's school at Tuskegee has trained thousands of Christian men and women to be leaders of the Negro people.

One of them, George Washington Carver, went to Tuskegee to study farming. Too much cotton growing in the south had made the soil poor and thin, and he wanted to find out how to enrich it. Carver learned that raising peanuts and sweet potatoes would make the soil fertile again. He found that three hundred products could be made from peanuts and sweet potatoes.

"What kind of products?" Michael looked doubtful. "Aren't peanuts peanuts, and sweet potatoes sweet potatoes?"

"Other people thought so until Dr. Carver showed them how to get flour, vinegar, and molasses from sweet potatoes; and cheese, milk, coffee, and soap from peanuts—to name only a few. He was a great scientist, and all his work was for other people."

Some of the Negro ministers trained by the Church went as missionaries to Africa to teach the people of their own race. Often they could do better than white missionaries, for many of the African people still thought that all white men were like the slave traders who had treated them so shamefully. They were afraid to trust them.

A hundred years went by and the world had changed. The Christian Church was no longer the Church of America and Europe alone. It was also "The Church of Christ in China," "The Church of Christ in Japan," and the "South India United Church." Where once the missionaries had counted a few hundred native Christians, there were now millions, with their own preachers, teachers, and doctors. This did not mean that all the work had been done or that help from Christian countries was no longer needed—far from it. The young native churches had to be strengthened in their task of reaching the people who still had not heard of Christ. But the Church in America and Europe saw new problems in these lands. These were problems of poverty and starvation among great masses of people; of wrong ways of living that led to sickness and crime; of millions of people who could not read or write. The Church must help solve these problems all over the world. It must work for a better life among all peoples if it would be true to the Master who said, "As you did it to one of the least of these my brethren, you did it to me."

Far away in the Philippine Islands an American teacher, Dr. Frank Laubach, had a plan. More than half the people in the world could not read or write, so he would teach them. But how could one man even begin to teach more than half the world's population? "Everyone," said Dr. Laubach, "who learns to read must teach someone else. This will go on and on until the whole world knows how to read and write!"

Dr. Laubach went to other countries: to India and Siam, to Africa and South America. Wherever people learned to read, the very first story they were taught to read was the story of Jesus.

"Now we really are up to our own day!" Michael exclaimed.

Mr. Wells nodded. "Yes—but we mustn't think of today as the end of the Church's story. We are part of a new beginning. Christian people everywhere must decide whether the Church shall lead or lag behind, in a world that is changing very fast."

As in the days when Luther reformed the Church, people are waking up and asking questions. They want the answer to their questions in deeds more than words. "What," they ask, "is the Church doing about the problems that we are facing today? What are Christians doing about the men, women, and children in foreign lands who are just as much their neighbors as those who live next door?"

The Church is finding out that it cannot lead people to love Christ unless it helps them in every part of their life. The Gospel of Christ must be taken into homes, schools, hospitals, prisons, slums. A Chinese bishop says that in the midst of strife and misery "many are turning to Christianity as the only hope. They look to it to point the way." A Japanese Christian minister also tells us, "From the imperial family down to the prisons the door is open wide to the Christian Gospel." And from deep in the heart of Africa comes the cry of an African chief, "The

Christian Church must work *twice* as hard to capture Africa for Christ, and it must be done *now* or it will be too late."

Christian churches of every name are answering: "We can do it. We can lead the world to Christ if we forget the things that divide us and think only of how we can work together. We must begin, like the early disciples, to meet together, break bread together, and pray together. God's Holy Spirit will come into our hearts as it did into theirs on the Day of Pentecost, and like them we shall go out to change the world."

So today a World Council of Churches has been formed to think and plan together for the good of mankind. It is a great Church family, united under one Father, God; one Leader, Jesus Christ; and one Spirit, working through them all to lead the nations in world-wide friendship and service for Christ.

"That makes me think of a hymn you all know," said Mother. "Do you remember?

"'In Christ there is no East or West,
In Him no South or North;
But one great fellowship of love
Throughout the whole wide earth.'"

"Jesus prayed that his followers might all be one," said Father, "and they started the Church that way."

"A lot of people have lived and died to make it grow," said Michael.

The Story Goes On

Our church bell is ringing!" Joan came racing in from the garden with a basketful of roses.

"Hurry up," Father called from the dining room. "Michael and I are ready for breakfast!"

A summer breeze stirred the curtains as the family sat down at the breakfast table. "The church bell has stopped ringing now," said Joan, "but it will begin again when it's time to start for church."

"It'll be nice to go to a real church again," said Michael.

"Yes, won't it? Last year on Children's Day the cornerstone had just been laid. Remember?"

"And Mr. Wells had just begun to tell us about the Church," added Michael.

"It was a good story, wasn't it?" said Joan. "I wish it could have gone on and on."

"I suppose," said Michael, "it really is going on—only we're writing the story now."

Joan opened her eyes wide as she thought about this. "Why, so we are!"

"I wonder—" Michael's face was a little more serious than usual—"if someone, a hundred years from now, will tell what we did in the story of the Church? We'd have to do something great like Paul, or Augustine, or Luther, or Livingstone, or—Marcus Whitman."

"Maybe we will!" Joan looked eager to start right off. Then she added, "But I suppose there have been millions and millions of people who have helped the Church grow, and no one knows even their names."

3303–02